Republicanism, Crime and Paramilitary Policing in Ireland, 1916–2020

For Órla, Cahir and Oisín

Studies in Irish Crime History

Republicanism, Crime and Paramilitary Policing in Ireland, 1916–2020

Brian Hanley

CORK UNIVERSITY PRESS

First published in 2022 by
Cork University Press
Boole Library
University College Cork
Cork T12 ND89
Ireland

Library of Congress Control Number: 2022936364

Distribution in the USA Longleaf Services, Chapel Hill, NC, USA.

British Library Cataloguing in Publication Data
A CIP catalogue record for this book is available the British Library.

ISBN 9781782055471

Printed by Hussar Books in Poland

Design and typesetting by Alison Burns at Studio 10 Design, Cork

Cover image: Provisional IRA colour party at Bodenstown, 1983.
(Photograph: Derek Speirs)

www.corkuniversitypress.com

Contents

Studies in Irish Crime History   vii

List of Abbreviations   viii

Acknowledgements   ix

Introduction   1

Chapter 1   **Policing the Revolution**   11

Chapter 2   **Control, Chaos and Criminality:**
            The Civil War and after   35

Chapter 3   **Rethinking and Re-organisation:**
            From the 1930s to the Northern War   59

Chapter 4   **Blurring of Boundaries?**   89

Epilogue   109

Notes   113

Bibliography   142

Index   155

Studies in Irish Crime History

SERIES EDITORS: Richard Mc Mahon and Ciara Molloy

This book series explores how crime history can offer new ways of understanding Irish society. It maps and critically engages with the actions and beliefs of those who often held a marginal position in Irish society, their relationship to the broader population and, crucially, their interactions with those in positions of authority. The history of the murderer, the prostitute, the thief, the bank robber, the vagrant, the white-collar criminal, among others, and their relationship to the police officer, the lawyer, the jury, the judge and the hangman will be explored to arrive at a deeper sense of the conflicts and contradictions that underpinned Irish life and continue to shape it into the present. The series also aims to explore the construction and meaning of key concepts such as 'crime' and 'evil' and the impact of such concepts on the individual, society and the state. In doing so, the series will embrace but also cut across key aspects of political, legal, economic, social and cultural history and raise questions about the nature of Irish society over time in fruitful and novel ways.

1. Brian Hanley, *Republicanism, Crime and Paramilitary Policing in Ireland, 1916–2020.*

List of Abbreviations

COCAD	Coalition of Communities Against Drugs
CPAD	Concerned Parents Against Drugs
DAAD	Direct Action Against Drugs
ICA	Irish Citizen Army
INLA	Irish National Liberation Army
IPLO	Irish People's Liberation Organisation
IRA	Irish Republican Army
IRP	Irish Republican Police
IRSP	Irish Republican Socialist Party
OASA	Offences Against the State Act
OIRA	Official Irish Republican Army
PIRA	Provisional Irish Republican Army
RAAD	Republican Action Against Drugs
RIC	Royal Irish Constabulary
RUC	Royal Ulster Constabulary

Acknowledgements

I would like to thank Richard Mc Mahon for the invitation to write this short book. Writing it was only possible through the generosity of other scholars, Sam McGrath, Patrick Mulroe, Terry Dunne and John Dorney in particular. I would also like to thank Breandán Mac Suibhne, Aoife Breathnach, Linda Connolly, Joe Mooney, Pádraig Yeates, Pádraig Óg Ó Ruairc, Roddy Hegarty, Barry Sheppard, Ciarán Murray, Tommy McKearney, Gerard Shannon, Peter Rigney and Tommy Graham for their help. Kate Manning and the staff at UCD Archives were, as always, a pleasure to work with. I have benefited greatly from the cutting-edge work being done online on sites such as *The Irish Story*, *Peelers and Sheep*, *Come Here to Me*, *East Wall for All* and the *Military Service Pensions Blog*. I also drew on the vivid local studies undertaken by John Borgonovo, John O'Callaghan, Adrian Grant, Michael Foy and others. This book was completed in the midst of the COVID-19 'lockdown' and as a result would simply not have been possible without the digitisation of the Bureau of Military History witness statements and the Military Service Pensions files. A generation of Irish historians owe a great debt to Cécile Gordon and the staff of the Military Archives. I also want to sincerely thank Richard Mc Mahon and Ciara Molloy for their careful editing and constructive criticism of the earlier drafts. Rob Devane, Joe Doyle and all at MAI helped keep me sane. Throughout the writing process I was greatly entertained by Cahir and Oisín, who raised my spirits whenever they slackened. The book could not have been completed without the support of Órla, who once again ensured that I got over the finish line.

Introduction

This book examines the relationship between Irish republicanism, policing and crime from 1916 to the present day. While there is little academic attention paid to this aspect of republican history, crime and policing arose as issues in every era of the IRA's existence. This book describes republican attempts to deal with crime during the War of Independence, the problems caused by the Civil War split and how the organisation grappled with accusations of criminality throughout much of the twentieth century. These questions emerged again with a vengeance during the modern Irish conflict after 1969 and persisted into the early decades of the twenty-first century. During this period, the perceived connection between the IRA and gangland crime also became established in both state discourse and popular culture, north and south of the border.

Indeed, the third series of RTÉ's hugely popular and critically acclaimed *Love/Hate* focused on the relationship between Dublin gangsters and republicans.[1] Shown during 2012, this series began with the kneecapping by the 'RA' (the IRA) of a gang member for drug dealing. The gang's leader, Nidge, is forced to meet the IRA to smooth things out. It transpires the kneecapping was a mistake, as the gang was paying protection money to the republicans. The IRA leader, 'Git' (whom we later discover had served a long jail sentence for Provisional IRA activities), decides to 'piggyback' on Nidge's drug importation route to bring in weapons. Git drinks heavily, snorts cocaine, brutally beats up a friend of Nidge's and

1

finally attacks and rapes one of the gang's girlfriends (all in the first episode). As a result, he is battered to death, establishing the season's main storyline. By the conclusion of the series Nidge manages to escape with his life only by agreeing to channel profits from his criminal enterprise to the 'RA' (who as the storyline develops we learn is the Continuity IRA, a 'dissident' group).[2] The series drew overwhelmingly positive reviews and it was notable that not one mainstream commentator thought the depiction of republicans to be unrealistic.[3]

The portrayal of republicans in *Love/Hate* fitted neatly into the genre of popular writing associated with journalist Paul Williams, whose *Badfellas*, 'the story of how Ireland lost its innocence and became a hotbed of gangsterism, murder and mayhem', was a bestseller in 2012. This book presented the modern IRA, in all its versions, as essentially another criminal gang.[4] Commentators such as Williams and Jim Cusack of the *Irish Independent* contend that republican opposition to the drugs trade is rhetorical and that the IRA 'tax' drug dealers but allow them to operate.[5] The showing of *Love/Hate* coincided with a series of events which, if anything, tended to confirm, in the public mind at least, this thesis. In September 2012, Alan Ryan was gunned down near his home in Dublin. As a leading 'dissident' who had served a jail sentence for participation in a Real IRA training camp, 31-year-old Ryan featured regularly in the media.[6] In a twelve-page supplement published on the first anniversary of his death, the *Sunday World* recounted how Ryan had 'become a dead man walking. Leading a group of terror thugs, he had lurched from one drug-dealing mob to the next demanding a cut of their profits, while threatening bloodshed and the full might of the new paramilitaries on those who refused.'[7] Ryan's 1,000-strong funeral saw a show of strength by the Real IRA, with men and women wearing paramilitary uniforms marching alongside the cortège and volleys of shots fired over his coffin. The oration was given by Colin Duffy from Lurgan, one of the most high-profile 'dissidents' in Ireland. Duffy attacked those who linked Ryan with crime, describing him as a 'brave Irish republican and fearless IRA volunteer'.[8]

In December 2012, 65-year-old Eamon Kelly was shot dead by the Real IRA, his killing regarded by many as retaliation for Ryan's. Kelly was reputedly a leading figure among Dublin gangsters and was looked upon as a mentor by younger criminals. In the early 1990s, he was jailed for organising one of the first large shipments of cocaine into Ireland. In his youth Kelly had associated with republicans.[9] During the 1980s he was reported to have carried out robberies with the Official IRA. He was also connected with the Irish National Liberation Army (INLA). To the surprise of many, Kelly's funeral saw an oration from 56-year-old Dessie O'Hare, the so-called 'Border Fox'.[10]

O'Hare had become notorious during 1987 when he kidnapped Dublin dentist John O'Grady. During more than three weeks of wild chases and gun battles, O'Hare evaded capture despite a major garda manhunt. Any public admiration for the daredevil nature of O'Hare's exploits was tempered by shock when two of O'Grady's fingers were hacked off and left in Carlow Cathedral.

O'Hare was eventually apprehended after being wounded at a roadblock, while an associate was shot dead. The revelation that one of O'Hare's gang had stabbed a man to death in a nightclub row just days before the kidnap of O'Grady was for most people proof of the criminal nature of their enterprise. Yet, O'Hare had been a member of both the IRA and the INLA and claimed his motivation was political. Sentenced to forty years in prison, O'Hare was released in 2006 and was soon associated by the media with gangland crime (he would be jailed again in 2019 for involvement in falsely imprisoning and assaulting a man).[11] At Kelly's funeral, O'Hare described the murdered man as a 'martyr' to the 'terrible beauty' of Ireland's 'freedom struggle'.[12]

In the United Kingdom, a clear narrative linking republicans to crime also formed part of the discussions around republican activity during the peace process. In 2005, the British government's Organised Crime Task Force stated that 'all paramilitary organisations in Northern Ireland are heavily involved in organised crime both as a means of raising finance for their organisations and for personal gain'. The Independent Monitoring Commission noted 'the tendency for republicans to predominate in cases of smuggling, armed robbery and fraud and for loyalists to specialise in drug crimes, intellectual property theft and extortion'.[13] The allegation that the IRA was motivated by criminal rather than political aims was also regularly aired throughout the Northern Ireland conflict. From the mid-1970s onwards British politicians habitually referred to the 'godfathers' of violence, a deliberate reference to the contemporary Hollywood Mafia blockbuster.[14]

Allegations of criminality can, in this sense, clearly be used as a political tool of delegitimisation by critics of the IRA, and governments and some state agencies may apply the label of 'criminal' to deny political motives to activists. In this context, republican military activity can even become synonymous with 'crime'. 'The IRA' or variations thereof has also been depicted as part of the criminal underworld in TV dramas such as *Sons of Anarchy*, *Boardwalk Empire* and *Peaky Blinders* and the classic British gangster movie *The Long Good Friday*.

In the face of these media and state allegations of criminality, all the armed republican groups claim political perspectives, historical lineage and forms of activism that set them apart from criminal organisations. Their supporters would assert that they inhabit a completely separate moral plane from criminal gangs, one explaining that 'you either despise criminality or you're not a republican'.[15] As Sinn Féin's newspaper *An Phoblacht* asserted when it dismissed what it called Paul Williams' 'latest work of fantasy', such allegations were 'hogwash' concocted by commentators for whom 'the IRA were always criminals'.[16] Their response was summed up by the chorus of Francie Brolly's 'H-Block Song':

I'll wear no convict's uniform,
Nor meekly serve my time
That England might brand Ireland's fight
Eight hundred years of crime.[17]

For republican prisoners, particularly those of the Provisional IRA and the INLA who undertook long prison protests and hunger strikes from 1976 to 1981, the accusation that they represented a 'criminal conspiracy led by Mafia-like godfathers' was met by a 'determination that neither they nor their liberation struggle were ever to be criminalised'.[18] Replying to accusations about involvement in crime during 2005, the Provisional IRA asserted that 'our patriot dead are not criminals. We are not criminals ... Ten of our comrades endured the agony of hunger strike and died defeating the criminalisation strategy. We will not betray their courage by tolerating criminality within our own ranks.'[19] There can be no doubt that there were long periods in which the IRA refused to endorse tactics such as robbery. Indeed, republicans have often assumed the status of upholders of the law, most obviously during the War of Independence (see Chapter 1) but also during and after the 'Troubles' in Northern Ireland (see Chapter 4). From this perspective, the IRA generally presents its activities as devoid of either criminal intent or associations.

Yet, republican attitudes to, and willingness to engage in, actions perceived to be criminal have also varied over the twentieth century. Republicans have sometimes endorsed activities that sizeable proportions of the wider population *and* some other republicans view as 'criminal'. Indeed, throughout its history, members of the IRA have often been divided over what constituted legitimate action. At times, such as during the 1956–62 'border campaign', involvement in robberies was considered deeply damaging to the republican cause, while at others, such tactics were justified as a necessity. The most iconic republican figure of the modern period, Bobby

Sands, took part in robberies of an insurance man and a shop on behalf of the IRA in the early 1970s.[20] From the Provisional IRA's point of view at that time, raising funds in this fashion was crucial. As a former Provisional IRA volunteer explained, funds (from robberies) 'would buy weapons, feed volunteers on the run, help look after the families of those in jail and keep the war machine ticking over'.[21]

Such contrasting perspectives on the definition of crime highlight, if nothing else, the obvious fact that crime is an often contested and elusive concept shaped and re-shaped, over time, by prevailing legal, political and cultural contexts. The media, state agencies and paramilitary groups are involved in a constant and divisive contest over the meaning of actions and events. This book traces, therefore, how these competing concepts of crime were applied to, and by, republicans in Ireland across the twentieth and early twenty-first centuries. It does not discuss the morality of or political rationalisation for armed campaigns, which may have involved activities that some view as 'criminal'. It explores instead how republicans have often grappled with the meaning of 'crime'. IRA concepts of criminality often did not differ much from broader society in seeing most forms of 'crime' as anti-social and deserving of punishment. Unlike some left-wing writers, republicans rarely justified crime by arguing that the perpetrators represented 'Robin Hood' figures or were engaged in what Eric Hobsbawm described as 'social banditry'.[22] Yet, they could also allow themselves scope for activity that others would regard as 'ordinary' crime rather than political action. In this sense, the book does not subscribe to a fixed legalistic definition of crime but allows for the fact that concepts of 'crime' can reflect prevailing but malleable norms shared across diverse social and political groupings. The book also explores how involvement in robbery and other forms of illicit fundraising can pose political and practical problems for republican organisations. As we shall see, depending on the context, they have dealt with this by denying any involvement in such activities at all or by contesting the very nature of what constitutes 'criminal' activity. This book focuses on involvement in what might be termed 'ordinary crime' by republicans, particularly robberies. This is not to deny political motivation for such activity but is a recognition of the fact that this aspect of republicanism is often overshadowed, in historical and sociological writing, by the more obviously political dimensions of IRA activity.[23]

There is now a wealth of primary source material from the Bureau of Military History and the Military Service Pensions files which allow us to access a forgotten world of policing and criminal activity during the Irish revolution. Though there are issues with oral histories collected decades after the event and with information supplied in order to gain pensions, the advantages of these sources include the revelation of attitudes and detailing of activities, as remembered by activists, that are ignored in most histories of the era. These archives need to be handled with care, but to deny their value in excavating the outlook and actions of IRA activists is to unnecessarily dismiss a rich and valuable source. The papers of senior republicans such as Richard Mulcahy and Maurice

Twomey also offer glimpses into this under-researched area. Source material from the 1960s onwards is scarcer and the tendentious, biased and partial nature of media coverage of the republican movement makes analysis more difficult. Recent work by Patrick Mulroe, Gearóid Ó Faoleán, Terry Dunne, John Dorney, Sam McGrath, Thomas Earls Fitzgerald, Pádraig Yeates, Linda Connolly, Kieran Glennon and others has been tremendously useful.[24] This book makes no claim to be the last word on the subject, but it is an attempt to throw light on an area largely neglected by historians.

Chapter 1

Policing the Revolution

I N JANUARY 1919 a new parliament, Dáil Éireann, representing an independent Irish republic, met in Dublin for the first time. Questions of crime and punishment rapidly came to the fore as the revolutionary administration attempted to assert its authority. Prior to the revolution, while heavily policed, Ireland was considered to have low rates of 'ordinary' crime. Many of the disturbances which concerned the authorities were agrarian or political in nature. In July 1920 a member of the British administration asserted that 'the amount of ordinary crime in Ireland is very small, there were only 450 prisoners in the country when they had the accommodation for 6,000'.[1] Nevertheless, in Dublin, a city with major levels of urban deprivation, the First World War witnessed an apparent rise in criminal activity. After 1914, offences carried out by 'juvenile gangs, often abetted by adults, such as housebreaking and robbery of coal trains, became common, along with fraudulent claims for Separation Allowances, theft of military property and increased desertion rates from the British armed forces'.[2] Indeed, during the Easter Rising, once it became apparent that the police were no longer in control of the streets, there was widespread looting. Detective Eamon Broy recalled 'bizarre sights … corner-boys wearing silk hats, ladies from the slums sporting fur coats, a cycling corps of barefooted young urchins riding brand new bicycles stolen from some of the shops, and members of the underworld carrying umbrellas'.[3] This reflected the poverty of the city, but also illustrated that criminals would take advantage of an absence of authority.

Crime, however, was not the main consideration on the minds of republicans when they launched their armed campaign and initiated a boycott of the police (the Royal Irish Constabulary (RIC)) during 1919. But these actions meant that soon 'large tracts of the country were not policed'.[4] Republicans noticed now that as 'no police duties, as these are understood in other countries, were being performed ... criminals were free to carry on their depredations against society'.[5] Joseph O'Connor noted that as the Dublin Metropolitan Police were becoming inactive, there was a 'great danger [the] criminally inclined element of the city would take advantage'.[6] Similarly, after February 1920 the RIC did not patrol Charleville in County Cork at night and as a result 'robberies were rife around the town and district'.[7] In the east Mayo area, the withdrawal of the RIC 'gave rise to another problem – that unruly elements among the people would have a free hand to indulge in their antics, such as petty robberies and the like'.[8] Republicans later explained how 'the neglect by the R.I.C. of ordinary police work had given to the criminal elements which exist in all societies a large measure of immunity'.[9] Indeed, by January 1920 there appeared to be an upsurge in crime, with reports of 'many more daring robberies' on a daily basis. The British press claimed that 'many of these outrages, notably in the Dublin area, are entirely unconnected with Sinn Féin'. While some violence was linked to labour disputes, 'organised bands are committing burglaries and highway robberies. These gangs call themselves by picturesque names, such as "Sons of Dawn" and "Knights of the Moon", and go about armed and masked, breaking into houses and stopping and robbing pedestrians'. Newspapers reported men entering pubs, farms and homes and forcing people to hand over money or possessions. Shops and post offices were also held up and vehicles and livestock stolen.[10] During 1920, bank raids started to become commonplace. There were a variety of factors at work, including increasing agrarian and industrial militancy and the willingness of those involved to use violence. In Britain, which also saw an apparent upsurge in violent crime, many blamed the 'thousands of neurotics ... created by the war'.[11] Certainly, war veterans featured in many incidents in Ireland as well, but the success of republicans in isolating the police through boycott was also relevant. One judge, noting what he called the 'immunity enjoyed by the criminal class', blamed the 'withdrawal by a large section of the community of that support of the law and its ministers which every citizen was morally and legally bound to afford'.[12]

As the IRA's armed campaign escalated, republicans noted that the withdrawal of the police had created a situation 'whereby robbery and those who lived on robbery thrived'.[13] By the winter of 1920 'criminals took advantage of the British curfew regulations to resume their attack upon society and were seldom molested by the British forces'.[14] Indeed, there was a suggestion that the 'number of large robberies indicated the presence of professional English criminals'.[15] The IRA felt forced to respond. Throughout 1919 local units began to undertake a policing role. This worked in tandem with the Dáil's construction of an alternative legal system, whereby Dáil courts were established in place of the existing British ones.[16] IRA officer Simon Donnelly explained how 'decrees in Republican Courts had to be enforced. In some cases, this entailed seizing of goods for non-payment of fines and so forth … decrees of Dáil Éireann also had to be enforced [as well as] many English laws retained for expediency'. These included dealing with 'illegal fishing, making of poteen, seizing of illegal stills, control of emigration, school attendance and cattle driving, all of which got somewhat out of hand'.[17] One account later stressed how 'the I.R.A., with the people on their side, addressed themselves whole-heartedly to their task. Malefactors were tracked down, arrested, convicted and punished; and stolen property was recovered and restored, often within twenty-four hours of the theft.'[18] In reality, IRA members were, for a variety of reasons, often reluctant to become policemen. One volunteer admitted that he 'had no idea how to investigate crime'.[19] Local responses varied, as did the types of problems faced.[20] Some welcomed the opportunity policing gave volunteers, Walter Brown asserting that 'it was good for them. It gave them work to do and was a decided change from the monotony of parading and drilling and helped to build an esprit de corps.'[21] However, sometimes only men 'unsuitable for military duties for one reason or another' were tasked with police work.[22]

It was not until the summer of 1920 that a formal Irish Republican Police (IRP) force, that included (in theory at least) non-IRA members, was established. From June 1920 each IRA unit was supposed to allocate a number of men in each area to this work.[23] In Dublin members of the small workers' militia, the Irish Citizen

Army (ICA) also undertook policing under the auspices of this force. Among other activities, their men captured a gang of 'common robbers' who had held up a shop in Sheriff Street.[24] Prior to the formal establishment of the IRP, IRA volunteers engaged with police work themselves. In Charleville, for example, the IRA set up a local 'vigilance committee' which had 'many encounters with would-be robbers before and after midnight' until the majority of these crimes ceased.[25] A pattern soon developed whereby 'parties of Volunteers used to arrest law breakers, take them to "unknown destinations" and impose fines after the case had been properly investigated'.[26] These 'unknown destinations' included isolated mountainside cottages, disused farmhouses, unoccupied 'big houses' and even an abandoned prison in Mullingar.[27] A shed in Ringsend was used to house some 'ugly customers' arrested by the IRA in Dublin's south inner city.[28] In Newcestown, County Cork, a vacant labourer's cottage was the local 'prison'.[29] Conditions for prisoners were rudimentary but do not seem to have been excessively harsh. Ernie O'Malley recalled how men guarding prisoners 'played cards with them, smoked, chatted and swapped stories'.[30] John Quinn, a 17-year-old Tyrone man accused by the IRA of stealing cash from a woman in Cookstown, was 'jailed' in a mountainside cottage. He recalled being 'well treated but we had to cook our own food; we got tea, bread, milk, potatoes and salt but had no butter or meat'.[31] Annie Deignan, a Sligo Cumann na mBan (republican women's auxiliary) activist, recalled that 'cooking was practically continuous' for both guards and prisoners being held near her home. Bridget Buckley had a similar experience during a long-running IRA investigation in north Cork.[32] However, many IRA units found having to hold prisoners a 'shocking nuisance', with manpower wasted on guard duty. Indeed, in one case when the RIC managed to rescue men being held by the IRA, the volunteers breathed a 'sigh of relief' to be rid of their captives.[33]

The extent to which IRA units embraced this policing role differed from area to area. In Limerick city they 'recovered stolen money and bicycles, regulated the opening hours of public houses, and curbed the menace of hurling on the roads'.[34] In Mayo the IRA received £600 from the Fishery Conservation Board for preventing poaching. The same unit also fined people for not having lights on their bicycles.[35] In many areas, pubs were issued with strict instructions on their opening hours and ordered not to serve drink on Sundays or church holidays.[36] The IRA boasted of the suppression of poitín-making in Donegal, Mayo, Galway and Clare.[37] In south Kerry, stills were seized, broken up and displayed outside local chapels after Sunday mass.[38] As a 'Pioneer all [his] life', Tyrone volunteer Thomas J. Martin was naturally 'against poteen makers' and led a major raid on a still at the Big Moss. Finding only one man present, Martin warned him that the 'penalty for this nefarious work was death – this was a little bit of a lie, but I wished him to disclose the names under threat'. Martin called upon six volunteers to come forward to be the firing party; he recalled that 'one of them said "Surely you're not going to kill him?" and I said "Of course I'm not; I am only going to scare him"'. After the poitín maker revealed the names of his collaborators, the IRA released him and destroyed the still.[39] Threats of violence seem to have been more common than the use of force. James Drew questioned three youths accused of stealing in Innishannon, County Cork, asserting that 'we did not use the third degree – they were not touched, but night after night they were examined'.[40] In contrast, Joseph Kinsella noted that 'a little rough handling' was needed to extract confessions from men who robbed an elderly woman in Dublin's Crumlin and were causing 'terror' in the locality. One of the suspects received '12 strokes of the cat'; a flogging.[41]

Punishments for petty offences varied. A tramp found guilty of stealing from a church collection box in Carlow was left alone on top of Mount Leinster.[42] A man who had broken into the home of a schoolmistress in Gorey, County Wexford, was forced to stand outside the local church during Sunday mass, flanked by two IRA men, wearing a placard reading 'Found guilty of attempted robbery'.[43] In Arklow, worshippers leaving mass observed a 'boy' tied to the chapel gates. Around the neck of the youth who was 'crying loudly' was a card bearing the words 'Caught by the I.R.P. stealing potatoes from the Convent garden'.[44] Fines or temporary detention were also common. In the case of what Simon Donnelly called 'incorrigible criminals … we adopted the practice of deporting them and issuing a warning that if they returned they would be shot'.[45] Donnelly complained that a request to allow flogging was turned down by the republican leadership as it was considered barbarous, but some units did flog miscreants believing that it was the 'only effective means of keeping serious crime in check'.[46] One 'particularly bad gang' in Dublin's south inner city had assaulted an IRA volunteer. They were arrested at gunpoint and their leader 'Hatchet Connor' forced to leave Ireland.[47] Being made to work on farms for a period was a common punishment in rural areas. Details of the sentences were often published in the local press, a Wexford volunteer, Francis Carty, explaining how he 'reported cases and supplied them to the local newspapers who published them in full, giving, of course, only the names of the persons charged and not the names of members of the Court'.[48] So in Killygordon, County Donegal, Patrick McGlichey was fined 7s 6d for assaulting a local farmer, while in Monasterevin, County Kildare, a labourer was fined 5s and barred from the vicinity of the local railway station after being accused of robbing bags of coal from there.[49]

One significant issue around the rise in crime was that much of it was 'perpetrated allegedly in the name of the IRA, the robbers claiming association with the IRA and in many instances getting away with it and the booty as well'.[50] In Shanagolden, County Limerick, 'local people were in dread of their lives' from one such gang. The IRA heard that livestock and farm produce were being 'stolen or seized by armed men at the point of a shotgun. All this was done in the name [of the] IRA ... we set about finding the culprits and succeeded in arresting a number of them. They were all farmers' sons and were not members of the IRA. We seized their arms and warned them of the consequences if they were caught again.'[51] There were similar cases in Offaly and in Waterford, where loyalist homes were robbed by a gang posing as the IRA.[52]

At the same time that the IRA was catching and punishing criminals, the British authorities charged republicans with criminal activity and with being little more than a 'murder gang'. Part of the republican policing effort involved countering these allegations by actually solving crimes. One of the most notable examples occurred in Millstreet, north Cork, during November 1919 when staff carrying £18,000 to the town's banks were held up and robbed.[53] The robbery was a nationwide sensation and many people assumed the IRA was responsible, a belief the British authorities encouraged. After carrying out their own investigation, a large IRA force occupied Millstreet during April 1920. After interrogating several suspects, they managed to secure £10,000 of the stolen money, which was returned to the banks. The culprits were forced to leave Ireland.[54] Áine Ceannt boasted that 'the British authorities were rather astounded at the success of this "illegal" police force'.[55] (The IRA also received a cash reward from the bank.[56]) There were similar, if smaller in scale, cases across the country. The IRA arrested two men who had robbed the manager of the Northern Bank in Skerries and returned most of the stolen cash.[57] In Schull, County Cork, the IRA gave back £500 to the Provincial Bank after apprehending the gang who had robbed it.[58] There was much positive local comment when the IRA in Roscommon returned £70 which had been stolen by thieves from a post office in Knockvicar during July 1920.[59] The IRA also recovered over £1,700 taken in a train robbery in Limerick that year and returned it to the railway company.[60]

There was particular kudos attached to winning the

confidence of those who were hostile to republicanism. During 1920 an armed gang looted the home of the aristocratic Duc de Stacpoole in Longwood, County Meath. IRA commander Seán Boylan assured de Stacpoole the raiders were not his men and promised to track down those responsible. The IRA captured the culprits, two of whom were stripped and flogged, and forced them to do farm work for a period. De Stacpoole's property was returned and he publicly thanked the IRA. Michael Collins told Boylan that de Stacpoole's statement had won favourable publicity for republicans internationally.[61] In Kilkenny a number of unionist businessmen and landowners praised republican police efforts on their behalf and contrasted them favourably with the RIC.[62] Galway IRA commander Joseph Stanford boasted that 'even the landlord class brought their cases to our courts'.[63] Lord Monteagle also commended the republican police for 'arresting burglars, punishing cattle-drivers, patrolling the streets [and] controlling the drink traffic'.[64] Kerry landowner Arthur Vincent told IRA chief of staff Richard Mulcahy that the 'Volunteers in my district are the people we owners of property look to for assistance; in my district they are doing their best to put down local robbing of orchards, etc'.[65] Archbishop Cohalan of Cork, often critical of the IRA, stated in December 1920 that the 'Volunteer police are now universally and deservedly popular and esteemed'.[66] The Dublin IRA were asked by Woolworths department store to keep their premises under observation in order to counteract a gang called the 'Sons of Dawn'.[67] Comprising young men from the inner city, the gang had robbed a number of shops in

Dublin. Several of them were captured by the IRA, tried, and forced to leave Ireland.[68]

There is no doubt that as part of the wider effort to create a counter-state, republican policing enjoyed popular support among a broad section of the population.[69] In its dealings with employers and landowners, the IRA was often very anxious to be perceived as even-handed. William Desmond explained that 'employers were treated as victims and given the same security as if they had been ardent supporters of the national cause; in other words, the IRA looked on all being equal citizens when it came to a question of justice being administered'.[70] This also reflected a strong sense of respectability that could make republicans intolerant of social outsiders such as tramps or 'tinkers'.[71] Republicans often displayed a contemptuous attitude towards certain types of people, especially poor town-dwellers.[72] Whether such perceptions affected their views on those who made up the 'lawless element of the population' deserves consideration.[73] As John O'Callaghan has astutely observed, 'IRA justice was not blind and not everyone was equal before IRA law'.[74] During 1920, the volunteers won much praise for forcing 'tramps and undesirables' to 'retire early' from fairs.[75] That summer the *Tuam Herald* had complained that 'since the great war the country has become infested with roving bands of tinkers who lead a sort of nomadic life, camping by the road side, and moving about from place to place as their fancy takes them, as uncontrolled and uncontrollable as the wind'. That newspaper noted approvingly how the IRA had dispersed 'tinkers' who had clashed with each other in Tuam.[76]

The *Tralee Liberator* also asserted that 'it is not easy to frighten a tinker especially when he is surrounded by his pals who usually carry with them soldering irons', but the volunteers in Killarney 'quietened them in a short time … when they realised that the Volunteers would not have any of their antics, the tinkers became almost lamb-like and followed out the instructions to leave the town peacefully'.[77] Roscommon IRA officer Thomas Lavin reflected that 'members of the Tramp or Tinker class, who often gave a bit of trouble … became very quiet. They knew what to expect when arrested by the RIC but what happened when arrested by the IRA was an unexplored region to them and they were not taking any chances.'[78] The IRA raided a 'tinkers' camp in Cork city searching for stolen goods'.[79] Ultimately, in the summer of 1921, the IRA in much of the south-west issued a general order that 'Tramps, Tinkers, etc., are rather a nuisance and a useful source of information to the Enemy. They are now prohibited in the area.'[80] Republicans generally saw crime as being caused by 'unruly elements and certain evilly disposed persons'.[81] The widespread agrarian and sectarian tensions that were evident across Ireland appear not to have influenced this view, but attitudes based on social class surely affected their responses.[82] There were nuances, however, in the IRA's approach. The republican movement generally took a benign view of labour activity and the IRA usually maintained a 'benevolent neutrality' during strikes. Land disputes were a different matter, however, with the Dáil suppressing small farmer agitation in the west of Ireland during 1919–20 and seeing so-called 'grabbers' as a threat to the national cause.[83]

John Borgonovo has shown that while the IRA was prepared to use deadly violence against informers (killing nearly 200 suspected spies), it rarely seems to have employed it against criminals.[84] Nevertheless, there were exceptions. In the case of the Millstreet robbers, a number returned to Ireland despite being deported. A 'difficult and dangerous' struggle ensued as the gang had a 'wide circle of relatives' in the area, ensuring them some local support.[85] The group's leader, Daniel Buckley, a publican and ex-soldier, even threatened the life of IRA commander Seán Moylan. Buckley was recaptured, tried and executed by the IRA, while several members of the gang were again forced out of Ireland.[86] Buckley's killing, however, was not publicised.[87] In Roscommon town two men were arrested by the IRA after a break-in at a shop. Despite questioning, they refused to admit their guilt and were released. One of them began to visit the RIC barracks regularly and so was abducted by the IRA and drowned, though it was admitted that it was unclear 'if he was giving information to the police'.[88] In Laois a labourer named Geoffrey McDonald was found guilty by a Dáil court of stealing horse harnesses and sentenced to deportation. But McDonald refused to leave the area and in January 1921 was shot dead by republicans during a raid on his home.[89] In Meath, IRA volunteer Mark Clinton was shot and killed while working on his uncle's farm. Local republicans alleged a criminal gang known as 'The Black Hand' were responsible.[90] William Gordon, a war veteran, was arrested by the RIC in connection with the shooting, tried but acquitted. After his release he was abducted by the Meath IRA, re-tried, found guilty and shot.[91] However, a rival republican account asserted that there was no 'Black Hand' gang and that Clinton was actually killed by Cavan IRA members who were in conflict with his family over land; tension between smallholders and large farmers was the cause. Gordon, as an ex-soldier (and Presbyterian), was simply a convenient scapegoat.[92] In Tipperary, a man due to be shot for robbery only survived because of the intercession of a local priest.[93]

One of the Dublin gangs broken up by the IRA, having carried out violent robberies of individuals during the winter of 1921, was also accused of several cases of 'indecent assault' against women.[94] However, Frank Henderson recounted just one rape case tried by a Republican court in Dublin (in which a priest was consulted on the moral implications of their decision).[95] Republican Seamus Fitzgerald knew of two cases of rape or attempted rape by Black and Tans in Cork city.[96] Until recently many agreed with the contention that during the Irish revolution 'the rape of women, like the murder of women, was not very common'.[97] Some maintain that sexual violence was rare during the War of Independence because crown forces did not want Britain's international reputation to suffer and had little to gain from the use of such tactics, while the IRA's actions were constrained by factors such as Catholicism and their dependence on community support.[98] However, recent research has suggested that sexual violence was far more prevalent than has been assumed but was 'quietly shrouded in forgetfulness' after the revolutionary period.[99] There was undoubtedly a sexual aspect to the murder by a British soldier of Kate Maher in Tipperary during December 1920, for instance. Maher, an unmarried mother of one and a farm servant, had been drinking with British soldiers in a local pub. Nobody was found responsible for her death.[100]

To fund the emerging counter-state the Dáil issued republican bonds, initially in Ireland and then most successfully in the United States, where $5 million was raised. In order to secure undercover bank accounts, the IRA was prepared to assassinate magistrate and investigator Alan Bell in March 1920. Republicans were worried that Bell's investigations would lead the British to the source of their funding.[101] But financing for the IRA itself was more problematic. The organisation constantly struggled to adequately arm itself. In May 1921 British intelligence speculated that the IRA was short of finance and that recent bank robberies were 'highly significant as indicating the necessity for obtaining money at all costs to continue the struggle'.[102] While some Dáil funds went towards weapons procurement, the majority of IRA units were expected to buy their own guns. But while robberies might have been an obvious way of doing this, the Volunteer journal *An t-Óglách* would later claim that 'the IRA never resorted to this method of obtaining funds … because they realised that the road to Irish freedom did not lie through the bankruptcy of the Irish people'.[103] Instead levies were imposed on local communities, though with mixed results.[104] Some local units *did* then carry out fundraising robberies, but usually in a very piecemeal and uncoordinated fashion. Michael Lynch recalled a 'really brilliant officer' in Ennis, who organised a post office robbery and 'took this money, believing it to be British Government money, for the sole purpose of buying arms for his Brigade. There was not one penny of it used for any other purpose, but I remember the consternation in GHQ when this was announced. The officer was suspended and threatened with very severe penalties for this breach of regulations.'[105] When the local IRA stole £400 in old age pensions from a train at Ballaghaderreen, County Roscommon, despite it being a 'welcome addition' to their funds it caused much internal dissension.[106] Pádraig Yeates has claimed that the purpose of some republican police work in Dublin was to help facilitate robberies. Joe McGrath, Sinn Féin TD and finance officer at Liberty Hall, received the money from these raids and passed it on to Michael Collins.[107] Citizen Army member Laurence Corbally and his father Richard were involved in several robberies of Dublin banks during May 1921, but it is not clear if these were authorised by their superiors.[108]

Examples of IRA members carrying out robberies for personal benefit are more common than cases where the proceeds reached headquarters. In early February 1918, two IRA officers robbed the manager of a bank in Ennistymon, County Clare, of £6,000. The men then took to wearing 'flashy outfits' and 'swaggered about the area from pub to pub more often than not under the influence of drink'. The failure of the local IRA to discipline them caused much bad feeling.[109] An IRA officer in west Waterford robbed several houses under the guise of raiding for arms. Expelled from Waterford, he took refuge with relatives in Cork, before being arrested for robbery there by the RIC.[110] A rent collector was robbed by IRA members acting for themselves in County Limerick.[111] Two Clare IRA members, who were active in their local unit, robbed Lahinch post office of £30. They were punished by being sent to work for local farmers for several weeks.[112] In Schull, two volunteers were court martialled for 'carrying out a robbery on their own'.[113] The homes of several Protestants were robbed in well-organised raids by armed men in west Cork. The 'terrified' victims were told that the IRA was responsible and there would be retribution if they complained. It was some time, therefore, before one of the homeowners contacted local republicans. Inquiries were made and it was discovered that a group of IRA members *were* responsible. These men were dismissed and punished.[114] The IRA in County Waterford brought an end to a spate of robberies, being carried out by a group of farmers' sons, by recruiting one of the men to their organisation, gaining his confidence and discovering the identity of the other culprits. Most of the stolen goods were recovered and returned to their owners.[115] In Charlestown, County Mayo, the IRA robbed nearly £5,000 from a bank in April 1921. This money was supposed to be used to purchase arms, but was instead divided up among the men involved.[116] James Redican, a 1916 veteran attached to the volunteers in Mullingar, robbed at least three banks in Dublin during the winter of 1920. Though Redican's comrades considered him a man with 'plenty of guts and courage [who] would be an asset to the [IRA] anywhere', the raids, carried out with his brother Thomas, were for his personal benefit.[117]

'Ordinary' criminals were also active, with several bank raids occurring in Dublin during which shots were exchanged with police. The Dublin Savings Bank lost £790 to a raid in November 1920, while its customers were also robbed. A publican named John Carroll led a gang that robbed several shops while claiming to be republican police. The Bank of Ireland's Pembroke branch lost £2,789 in a raid in November 1920 and £1,286 in another in February 1921. The National Bank lost £8,000 in robberies in the first half of 1921 alone.[118] Belfast was engulfed in inter-communal violence from the summer of 1920. In the midst of this, there were numerous, usually small-scale, robberies, such as the hold-up of a spirit grocer in Ballymacarret and the robbery of a warehouse in the city centre in early 1921.[119]

Members of the crown forces also took advantage of the confusion to commit crimes. In October 1920, Auxiliaries robbed a creamery at Kells. In December, a group of Black and Tans robbed a bank in Strokestown, County Roscommon.[120] In January 1921, James McCullough, a member of the newly formed Ulster Special Constabulary, was shot dead by police in Clones while taking part in an armed robbery of a grocer's.[121] The only Black and Tan executed during the period, William Mitchell, went to the gallows in April 1921 for the murder of a magistrate during a robbery of a private home in Wicklow.[122] Just as criminals sometimes pretended to be the IRA, 'bogus Black and Tans' were also active.[123]

There is little evidence of interaction between the IRA and the criminal underworld. Sinn Féin TD Phil Shanahan ran a pub in Dublin's Foley Street, the heart of the notorious 'Monto' district. Dan Breen claimed that the 'lady prostitutes' of Dublin's inner city used to 'pinch guns and ammunition' from the British forces, leaving them for the IRA at the pub. The same women also supplied intelligence to republicans, without expecting payment.[124] Yet, the IRA's own notions of respectability made such contacts problematic. Prostitutes, and even poor inner-city women more generally, were often suspected of being close to the British military.[125] The IRA's international operations presented more likely opportunities for such interaction. Local units in Ireland often had to make these foreign contacts independently of HQ. They found themselves having 'to frequent very dangerous places patronised by a rough element of society' and dealing with 'East End crooks' on occasion.[126] In London, James Delaney recounted how an Irish bookie with criminal connections introduced him to a 'Jewman' bookmaker named Ginger Barnett and a mixed-race gang leader known as 'Darby the Coon'. With them he developed a network for moving guns to the IRA in his native Kilkenny. Delaney purchased these weapons from African and Chinese sailors.[127] Another London IRA member, Denis Carr, with the aid of funds raised in Ireland, 'was in a position to negotiate with such criminal gangs as "the Titanics" in the "Nile", London, the "Sabinis" of Clerkenwell, an Italian mob, and the Birmingham mob. Through these, [he] made contact with a crook arms dealer in the Hackney Road, and through him was able to tap an unlimited source of ammunition and guns.'[128] Denis Kelleher of the Cork IRA said that their best London contact was 'a Jew named "Ginger"

[who] lived near Whitechapel station ... He was our main source of supply and he would deal only with myself. I had to go there 2 or 3 times a week, and we paid £2 or £3 a weapon.'[129] Richard Walsh carried out extensive smuggling on behalf of the Mayo IRA in Britain. One of his London sources was 'what was known as a "fence" – a dealer in stolen goods – and jewellery was one of his specialties'.[130] A London policeman, Denis Sugrue, operated as an intelligence officer for the IRA. He recruited three 'underworld agents' from criminal contacts to help him source arms.[131] James Cunningham, a Birmingham IRA member who had been held in Winson Green prison, recalled how 'the knowledge I gained of the underworld stood me in good stead, as it was a great source of "stuff"'.[132] The IRA managed to steal machine guns from a depot in Gateshead. Gilbert Barrington recalled that to move the weapons 'a horse and cart had to be hired from a shady character ... a member of [the] Askew Road Gang, who were of the underworld type'.[133] In Sheffield, Joe Good also recalled how 'we, at one time, rubbed shoulders of necessity with a criminal ring'.[134]

In moving weapons through ports across Europe and North America the IRA was often dealing with elements it would have avoided in Ireland itself. In Hamburg one contact was described as a 'bit of a booze hound type that would do any job if paid for it'.[135] In Liverpool, a key centre for IRA smuggling, one officer recalled how, as this was 'the period of Prohibition in the USA, many of the seamen supplemented their pay by carrying whiskey to New York'.[136] Another sailor was said to be willing to 'do anything for money, was a gambler, and a general all round rough character'. A seaman who played an important role in helping to spirit de Valera to America 'cared for neither God nor man. One thing he liked, however … was to see the police get the worst of it always.'[137] Entering this world brought dangers, however. Richard Walsh estimated that of the money allocated for arms purchases in Britain, a 'large sum', perhaps '£10,000 to £12,000', went unaccounted for.[138]

Police work featured far more in the day-to-day workings of the IRA between 1919 and 1921 than is usually imagined.[139] Indeed, filling the vacuum left by the retreat of the RIC was a significant part of the republican effort to establish a counter-state. Crucially, in many areas the IRA had the 'sympathy of the public, which is a great asset, and something the R.I.C. never possessed'.[140] But policing was never the IRA's primary purpose. Indeed, during September 1920 *An tÓglách* complained that in certain areas IRA units were using such tasks to avoid conflict with the enemy.[141] It claimed that 'in some places which are almost blank on the war map a great deal of arresting criminals, closing public houses, suppressing poitín stills and the like by Volunteers is reported. This is all good and necessary work; but it looks as though in such places Volunteers were allowing police work, which is only a secondary duty, to monopolise their attention and divert them from what is their primary work and the real object of their existence – to wage war against the enemy …'.[142] Further reorganisation of the police took place in June 1921 when it was decided that a 'police force to the number of ten in each Company area' be detached from the volunteers but backed up by them if necessary. Dublin officer Simon Donnelly was placed in charge of the force. New general orders to re-organise a distinct republican force were issued in November 1921, by which time a truce had been in place for several months and the leadership of the Dáil was in talks to bring about a settlement.[143] However, the truce period was to bring new problems, with an upsurge in criminal activity, alongside a deepening crisis for the IRA.

Chapter 2

Control, Chaos and Criminality: The Civil War and after

THE *EVENING HERALD*'s euphoric front-page coverage of the 'handover' of Dublin Castle to republican forces in January 1922 was accompanied by a report of a wild gun battle in Phibsborough between armed motor thieves and pursuing police.[1] The truce period had seen an upsurge in almost all varieties of crime. Republicans cooperated for a period with the crown forces to combat this, but tensions over the treaty and the IRA split introduced another dimension to the problem. The Civil War saw the Free State government use accusations of criminality to delegitimise republicans. But state forces were also implicated in criminal acts, both during and after the conflict.

During August 1922, Michael Collins wrote to Richard Mulcahy to complain about 'the wretched Irish Republican Police system [and] the awful personnel that was attracted to its ranks ... the lack of construction and the lack of control in this force have been responsible for many of the outrageous things which have occurred throughout Ireland'.[2] By then, Collins was engaged in a war against his former comrades and indulging in revisionism regarding what until recently had been a highly praiseworthy force. In the interim between the truce and the beginning of the Civil War, armed crime had escalated. Both pro-treaty and anti-treaty factions, along with members of the crown forces and civilians, engaged in criminal activities, while strikes and land disputes were often violent. In the midst of this a completely new police force was being established, the Civic Guards, which began recruiting in February 1922. But their rejection by the anti-treaty IRA meant that policing was initially confined to pro-treaty areas. The new police were also wracked by tensions over the enlistment of ex-RIC officers, resulting in a mutiny taking place at the Kildare depot during the summer of 1922. The force was not in a position to deal effectively with the increase in crime.[3]

As early as September 1921, *The Irish Times* reported 'another daring bank robbery' of £500 in Rathgar, with the raiders not bothering to disguise themselves.[4] The republican police were kept busy throughout the winter. In Youghal, County Cork, they were now based in a former RIC barracks. As well as recovering stolen goods and livestock and guarding the local banks, they also punished a 'bunch known as The Black Hand gang' by chaining them to the railings of the local church.[5] In Cork city, £1,000 worth of stolen jewellery was returned to Egan's stores. A gang in Limerick who robbed and assaulted 'young girls in the street' was broken up. In the same city, goods stolen from railway stores were recovered and returned.[6] During this period, the republican police cooperated with British forces. Republicans patrolled with British soldiers in north inner-city Dublin and tracked down a sniper who was targeting troops. The gunman was given twenty-four hours to leave the country or be shot. In the same area clashes between troops from the Royal Barracks and local youths threatened to develop into a riot in Smithfield. The IRA intervened, informing the British they could stand down. They then held up the youths at gunpoint, disarmed them and warned them they would be shot if they did not disperse.[7] In one instance a car stolen from a barracks in Tipperary was even 'restored to the Black and Tans'.[8] A similar sense of even-handedness was on display in Sligo when a 'valuable terrier' belonging to a British officer, believed to have strayed, was returned to its owner.[9] In Armagh a professional gang was stealing money and foodstuffs from the town's shops. The RIC district inspector approached IRA officer John McCoy and asked for cooperation in apprehending them. The IRA was able to gather enough information to ensure arrests but wanted an agreement from the police to release republican prisoners first. Tensions over the treaty ultimately meant that the deal collapsed.[10]

British servicemen were implicated in a number of cases. Republican police made a major effort in Dublin to track down a gang of 'gentlemen cracksmen', largely made up of British deserters (but including at least one republican), who carried out two armed wages raids in the winter of 1921. Investigations into their activities found that 'Claude Gunner's gang' had planned robberies of, among others, Thomas Cook's travel agency and the Tedcastle McCormick payroll. They then intended to target several banks before retiring with the proceeds to England. The gang was tracked down, apprehended by the IRP and held in the Columkille Hall in Blackhall Street (one of a number of premises used by republicans for holding criminal suspects during this period) before being handed over to the British military.[11]

The IRP was also increasingly given a public order role. They were praised for the way they 'exercised a salutary control over the rowdy element in Sligo on Christmas Eve … there was a marked absence of the disgraceful scenes of drunkenness and disorderly conduct which occurred in the town during recent weekends'.[12] In Dundalk, revellers ignored RIC patrols, taunting them that 'the IRA police are doing duty now'.[13] However, the use of republican police during strikes drew criticism from labour activists, who alleged that they had acted for employers during disputes in Dublin and Kilkenny. Indeed, in Tipperary republican police fired shots over the heads of strikers during a creamery occupation and confiscated and burnt a red flag.[14] One left-wing newspaper contended that the 'function of the I.R.P. is that of all Capitalist police forces, to protect property'.[15] But the republican police were hard-pressed to deal with what Simon Donnelly in February 1922 described as the 'wave of crime which began about three months ago and which has been caused by numerous armed bands operating all over Ireland'.[16] *An t-Óglách* too lamented that 'crimes of violence are unfortunately all too rife in certain parts of the country' and that the disturbed situation was one in which the 'criminal elements which exist in every community will strive to take advantage'. It warned that the army would make the 'sternest efforts' to 'stamp out the activities of lawless offenders'.[17]

In Dublin there had been several armed robberies of 'amazing audacity' in early 1922. Shots were exchanged with raiders who had stolen £3,000 from a jeweller's and who were captured after a chase involving both republican and Dublin Metropolitan Police.[18] By February, routine policing activities for the IRP included: guarding the Bank of Ireland at Elphin on market day; guarding a bank at Abbeyfeale for a week; investigating a spate of robberies of Drogheda shops; investigating the theft of a car at Kilmallock; arresting four Limerick men over a bank robbery in Croom; arresting two men in Castleblayney over the robbery of a salesman and searching for 'marauders' who were raiding farmhouses around Ballybofey.[19] Nevertheless, crime seemed to flourish. In Cork, 'large-scale armed robberies became common … though they had previously been extremely rare'.[20] A 'cool' robbery netted £2,000 in a wages snatch in the city during March.[21] Two banks in Sligo were robbed of £13,000 on 13 February. There were 331 raids on post offices alone between 23 March and 19 April 1922.[22] Dublin saw 479 armed robberies during that year. In March, Max Green, head of the Irish Prison Board, was shot dead on Molesworth Street when he tried to stop two men who had snatched a payroll.[23] A man named Anthony Walsh was shot and killed after he allegedly demanded money from Lord Massey at Killakee House, Rathfarnham.[24] (There was government intervention to prevent Massey facing charges.[25]) Belfast, wracked by violent sectarian conflict for two years, saw almost 'daily' armed robberies of shops and pubs, which contributed to the city's sense of 'lawlessness'.[26] Republicans were responsible for at least some of these. In June 1922 a bakery manager named Edward Devine was shot dead during an IRA robbery of his workplace on the Springfield Road. Devine's death caused 'widespread horror' among the local nationalist community.[27]

As the split over the treaty became increasingly bitter, Collins and his allies placed the blame for this lawlessness on their republican opponents.[28] The reality was more complex. IRA discipline had notably declined during the winter of 1921. As early as August, Simon Donnelly had warned that 'it is very plain that quite a number of men, and in some cases officers, are indulging in excesses which do not tend to maintain the good name of the Army', but he had excused this as the 'natural tendency' of men who had been fighting to 'enjoy themselves during the Truce'.[29] But Seán Moylan recalled that 'in public houses, at dance halls [and] on the road in "commandeered" motor cars' some republicans 'pushed the ordinary decent civilian aside and earned the IRA a reputation for bullying, insobriety and dishonesty that sapped public confidence'.[30] Both sides of the republican split accused each other of criminality. Collins would describe much anti-treaty activity as 'largely mere brigandage' carried out by 'criminal riff-raff, robbers and cut-throats'.[31] Kevin O'Higgins would later suggest that what was facing the Free State was 'less and less a question of war and more and more a question of armed crime'.[32] Republicans, for their part, described the Free State army as being made up of 'the tramp, the tinker and the brute' and recruits 'from off the street corners'; people who were prone to criminality themselves.[33] The reality was that members of both factions were taking advantage of the unsettled conditions even before the Civil War.

In early February 1922, £5,195 was taken from the Hibernian Bank at Charlestown, County Mayo.[34] When the IRA investigated, they found that the raid had been carried out by their own men, who had also robbed a bank in the town the previous year. The group, which included some of the 'head men' in the local IRA, claimed that they had forwarded £1,000 to GHQ but received no arms in return. One of those involved subsequently joined the Free State army and hence 'got away' without further punishment. (£3,097 was recovered and returned to the bank.[35]) East Waterford was plagued by gangs claiming to be republican police, who entered homes and stole valuables. One set of bank robberies was found to have been carried out by senior IRA officers in the region. The men were tried at Stradbally and sentenced to ten years' deportation. Some, instead, went to Dublin and joined the new National Army, among them Michael Bishop, serving as a commandant with Free State forces in Kerry.[36] John Cox, a republican policeman, was shot dead during a robbery in Lanesborough in April 1922. The raiders, all Free State soldiers, were captured in nearby Roscommon. After the onset of civil war, the men were released and 'assisted the National [Army] during hostilities'.[37] Patrick and Thomas Dunleavy had been senior IRA officers in east Galway. They were suspected of a series of bank and post office raids in the Tuam area in the spring of 1922, but both men joined the Free State army in September that year, leading to suspicion that they 'joined the Army with a view to the continuance of [this] policy under the protection of a uniform of a soldier of the State'.[38] A group of Free State officers were later charged with a series of armed robberies carried out in Castlebar during April 1922.[39] The anti-treaty IRA were also certainly involved in some of the raids. One of their volunteers, John Bergin, a labourer from Templemore, County Tipperary, was killed after a robbery, supposedly following a dispute among the raiders.[40]

The overall atmosphere contributed to demands for the restoration of order. In Cork city, 'personal scores were settled and mercenary criminals enjoyed an open field'.[41] The ferocious anti-Catholic violence across the new border saw the arrival of refugees and a desire for revenge among some nationalists. Those perceived to be southern unionists were sometimes targeted for raids and robberies and real fear existed in isolated Protestant communities.[42] Pro-treaty polemicists increasingly charged their republican rivals with sectarian animosity towards Protestants and of using the unsettled conditions as an excuse to rob them.[43]

In reality, a myriad of factors were at work, though religion was certainly among them.[44] Sectarianism influenced criminality on both sides of the new border, including some cases of sexual violence. Anti-treaty IRA members in Tipperary were involved in the brutal rape of a Protestant woman, Eileen Biggs, during a raid on her house. Her husband was shot and critically wounded. There was another vicious sexual attack on two Catholic women by Special Constables in south Armagh during the spring.[45] By the conclusion of the Civil War, the Free State army was implicated in a number of cases of sexual violence. In at least one case an anti-treaty Cumann na mBan activist was raped by army officers.[46] Linda Connolly, Lindsey Earner-Byrne, Gemma Clark and Mary McAuliffe have all investigated various forms of violence directed at women in this period; it is clear, as discussed in Chapter 1, that the scale of this has been previously underestimated.[47]

The anti-treaty forces formally authorised bank raids in May 1922. On 1 May a coordinated series of robberies was undertaken on the Bank of Ireland, which netted more than £50,000. By breaking with the new administration, the anti-treatyites no longer had any access to funds, while Free State soldiers were now receiving a wage and had food and lodgings. The raids, carried out by a force which considered itself the army of the republic, were seen as a military necessity. As Francis Carty explained, 'the problem of supporting the men in the barracks was pretty serious and at about this time the Four Courts [where one faction of the anti-treaty IRA leadership were based] sent out instructions that visits should be paid simultaneously to branches of the Bank of Ireland throughout the country and that whatever money was available should be commandeered ... I paid a visit to the Bank of Ireland in New Ross and took from the Manager £5,000'. Another unit took £11,000 from the bank's branch in Wexford town. In both cases a receipt, stating the officer's name and rank, was left with the bank manager. The money was handed over to a senior officer to be transferred to the republican leadership in the Four Courts. An amount was retained to supply provisions for the local units. Anti-treaty IRA guards were placed on the banks during this period and the officer claimed that the managers thanked the IRA for 'the manner in which we were preserving law and order in the area'.[48] However, others viewed the raids as more significant as they 'precipitated ... the first serious clash between the rival groups in the army ... The Bank of Ireland was the official treasurer of the Treaty party and the raids were all carried out in daylight ... these raids were undoubtedly the first operations of what we can describe as the Civil War'.[49] The pro-treatyites roundly condemned the robbery of the 'property of the people of Ireland' and stressed that this had never been a tactic resorted to by the IRA prior to the truce.[50] There was also a human cost. A woman, Mary Ellen Kavanagh, and a child, Esther Fletcher, were shot dead in crossfire between raiders and Free State troops in Buncrana after a bank robbery there.[51]

The IRA also carried out fundraising raids in Glasgow, Brentford and Manchester during the spring and summer of 1922.[52] Just £244 was taken in a raid at Prestwich in July, with one of those involved, a miner called Bartley Igoe, asserting that the '"dough" was taken [to] Dublin'.[53] However, Igoe and a comrade were captured, while two other raiders were deported back to Britain from the Free State. The four men served seven years in prison.[54] The anti-treaty rationale for bank raids was to regard them as part of a well-ordered military effort. But by the time the Civil War began there was often little indication of who was doing the robberies or why they were being carried out. Occasionally, they appeared to take place in tandem with the war, as when £2,000 was stolen from banks in Monaghan in July 1922, coinciding with attacks on Free State positions in the town in which a soldier was killed.[55] But following an investigation ordered by anti-treaty commander Frank Aiken, it was discovered that the robberies had been unauthorised. While £130 was returned to the Ulster Bank, some of the men involved fled the country with the rest of the money.[56]

The IRA's need to secure supplies also meant that goods of all types were requisitioned from shops. Such operations had been taking place since the summer of 1922, but in early September IRA units were 'authorised to raid big Unionist Firms and other anti-Irish Firms … for equipment, which will be useful for our flying columns and action Battalions', namely 'boots, leggings, trench coats, socks, underwear and military equipment'. The raids were supposed to be conducted 'very cautiously and quietly'.[57] But to the general public they looked like armed robberies and the definition of 'anti-Irish' could be very broad, as could the size of the business targeted. A raid of Fay's store in Edenderry, County Offaly, in September 1922 saw cakes, cigarettes, tobacco and clothing taken, while armed men who raided the home of J.L. Swift near Mullingar took his Brownie camera, silver kitchen utensils and other goods.[58] There was a realisation that such tactics could alienate the public. In September 1922 the IRA in Wexford were warned that 'it is not deemed wise to seize … Post Office cash and stamps and you will see that no such raids are carried out in your area'.[59]

Anti-treaty IRA commander Liam Lynch admitted that in some areas 'drunkenness, boisterous conduct while under the influence of drink, interference with or attempts to intimidate or terrorise the civil population' had damaged relations with civilians.[60] But as the anti-treaty position worsened, there was a turn to more destructive tactics. In an effort to disrupt the collection of 'enemy revenue', in December 1922 the IRA ordered that 'all post offices will be continually raided; stamps and money seized and all documents burned'.[61]

In early January 1923 an anti-treaty column, based in the Arigna mountains and short of food and resources, carried out a raid on Ballyconnell, County Cavan. One IRA volunteer, Michael Cull, was shot dead while robbing the town's post office. Cull had been killed by a Free State intelligence officer, but his comrades blamed townspeople.[62] They returned a month later, robbing £200 from the Ulster Bank branch and stealing cash and goods from several shops. But their motivation was also revenge, and a shop assistant called William Ryan was shot dead while the owner of the Ovens and Richardson department store was wounded. Three shops were destroyed and homes associated with Free State supporters attacked.[63] Such attacks only reinforced the Free State's assertions that the anti-treatyites were criminals. Those convicted of taking part in armed robberies could face a death sentence under the state's draconian security legislation. In March 1923, IRA volunteers Luke Burke and Michael Grealy were executed in Mullingar. They had been involved in the robbery of two banks at Oldcastle, County Meath. But because the robberies were unauthorised, neither man was included in the IRA's roll of honour.[64] In contrast, three young Offaly IRA men, William Conroy, Patrick Cunningham and Columb Kelly, who were executed at Tullamore in January 1923, received official recognition from their organisation. But they had actually been suspended from the IRA at the time for participation in 'minor robberies' including burglaries.[65] Liam Lynch had stressed that 'robbery will be sternly suppressed and persons falsely representing themselves to be soldiers of the [IRA] will be dealt with summarily'.[66] In November 1922, Patrick Kennedy, accused of being a 'spy and robber', was shot and his body left outside Portroe church, near Nenagh.[67]

But non-political criminals and opportunists continued to take advantage of the chaos. In the early stages of the Civil War even areas nominally under Free State control saw many robberies. In July 1922, Nellie McDonagh of Riverstown, County Sligo, was shot dead by a group of teenagers who raided her home.[68] One group of robbers who were captured near Strandhill in the county had been pursued by both the anti-treaty IRA and state forces. When arrested they asserted that they were 'Bolsheviks from the Ox Mountains and are starving'.[69] A shopkeeper in Annaghdown, County Galway, abandoned his business and took his family to Galway city after recurring raids in which food, drink and money were stolen from him.[70] There were almost daily cases of people, such as an 'aged farmer' near Carrickmacross or the Poor Law relief officer in Doon, County Limerick, being held up and robbed of relatively small amounts of money.[71] The payment of pensions was suspended in much of Leitrim because of continual raids on post offices.[72] In Dublin three policemen were held up and £700 in wages for the DMP stolen by armed men.[73] In east Donegal there had been a wave of robberies in the early stages of the war and the area remained disturbed. In March 1923, soldiers arrested a number of drunk men at a market fair in Creeslough. Later that night shots were fired at their barracks, killing Captain Bernard Cannon. Assuming that it had been an IRA attack, four republican prisoners were executed at Drumboe in reprisal. In fact, the Creeslough shootings were most likely carried out by friends of the arrested drunks.[74] Meanwhile, the anti-treatyites blamed a 'gang of robbers' led by an ex-IRA officer for terrorising people 'particularly the Unionist classes' in the Glen of Aherlow. When the IRA broke up this gang, the robbers supplied information to Free State forces which led to the death of senior officer Denis Lacey in February 1923.[75]

Anti-treaty IRA members did carry out robberies for their own purposes. In October 1922 an active service unit in Dublin was disbanded because of its coopera-tion with a civilian 'robber gang'.[76] But the state forces faced similar problems. The Protective Corps, a paramil-itary police unit set up to guard government offices in Dublin, had been detailed to defend cinemas and theatres. By 1923, members of this unit were extorting protection money from these businesses, threatening that unless paid off they 'would do the hold-ups themselves'.[77] Some of the IRA's operations were also misinterpreted as robberies. In April 1923, James Tierney was shot dead with his own gun after being tackled by a customer during a raid on a tobacconist's on Dorset Street. While assumed to have been a robbery, the IRA in fact suspected Free State intelligence was using the shop.[78] There was also confusion after the shooting dead of Patrick Cosgrave, the uncle of the Free State president W.T. Cosgrave, in September 1922. Cosgrave was killed, it appeared, in an 'attempt to frustrate an armed robbery' at a relative's pub. But army intelligence suspected that republicans had deliberately targeted him.[79]

Overall, the Civil War saw the continuation of a propaganda campaign by the pro-treaty side to label their opponents as criminals. Indeed, accusations of banditry were also made against those taking part in strikes and land disputes. Yet, members of the state forces were often as likely as republicans to engage in robberies. Untangling responsibility for the myriad of such activities during the period after the truce is very difficult. What is certainly true is that anti-treatyites authorised bank robberies in May 1922, which marked a significant development in the republican attitude to such activities.

The Civil War ended with an IRA ceasefire on 24 May 1923, though violence continued throughout the winter with civilians, republicans, soldiers and gardaí all killed in this period. There were a variety of culprits, though the government continued to blame the IRA for almost all violence; meanwhile republicans noted that the abduction and murder of activists had continued *after* the ceasefire.[80] There were also 210 armed robberies in Dublin alone during 1923.[81] Just six days after the ceasefire, Joseph O'Rourke and Michael Murphy were executed in Tuam after being found guilty of a bank robbery in Athenry a week earlier.[82] The men were not claimed as IRA volunteers.[83] A hangover from the other civil war, north of the new border, was felt in May 1924 when Michael Pratley was hanged in Belfast. Pratley, a tailor, had shot a man dead during a wages robbery. Though a member of the IRA (and also initially charged with the murder of W.J. Twaddell, MP in June 1922), the raid he took part in was not authorised.[84] It was not only the state that deployed the ultimate sanction against those accused of criminal activities. In July 1923 Philip Doyle, an IRA member who had recently escaped from jail, was shot dead. A label attached to his body read, 'Shot by I.R.A. Convicted robber'.[85] Doyle was killed because of his involvement in the wounding of a garda sergeant who had refused to hand over his bicycle to the IRA. Doyle's killing caused much controversy among his comrades. Another volunteer was involved in the incident but allegedly 'was not asked one question on the matter', let alone punished.[86] The former commander of the IRA's 2nd Dublin Brigade, court-martialled in December 1923 over his keeping £1,200 from a robbery at Blessington, faced no such drastic punishment.[87] Doyle may have been shot because the IRA was sensitive to charges of attacking unarmed gardaí, but the inconsistent nature of its punishments probably encouraged others to take advantage. Garda commissioner Eoin O'Duffy (admittedly a biased observer) alleged that one anti-treatyite, by the late 1920s a Fianna Fáil representative on Clare County Council, had stolen 'over £12,000 from local banks, which he never either returned or accounted for to de Valera, the IRA, or anyone else'.[88] Christy Crothers of the Citizen Army was disgusted, on release from internment, to find that a 'certain officer and certain men' in the ICA in Dublin had 'disgraced its name' by becoming a criminal gang.[89]

Though the authorities blamed the 'Irregulars' for each and every armed crime, it is clear that many incidents involved members of the state forces in the immediate post-Civil War years. The several robberies that featured fatal violence in the short period between 1923 and 1924 illustrate this. Tom Fitzgerald, a detective (and IRA veteran), was shot dead by bank raiders in a gun battle at Castleknock in October 1923.[90] A month later a 21-year-old unemployed man, Patrick Kelly, was killed by detectives after an attempted robbery in Ballsbridge.[91] In early 1924, Garda Michael O'Halloran was shot dead after a bank raid in County Wicklow. Those involved in the Castleknock shoot-out were Free State soldiers, one of whom, William Downes, was hanged for murder.[92] Both men arrested for the Wicklow robbery were also former officers in the National Army.[93] One of them, Felix McMullen, was hanged for the murder of Garda O'Halloran.[94]

No fewer than 900 soldiers in the National Army were charged with various forms of criminal activity between 1922 and 1924.[95] Some of these men were IRA veterans, others former British soldiers. Michael Watchorn was jailed for robbing a pub in Dublin in December 1923.[96] James Freyne, a commandant in the army, along with two fellow officers, held up and robbed £50 from a man in Drumcondra.[97] John Reynolds, a wounded Longford veteran of the War of Independence, was jailed in 1925 for the robbery of a woman's home. He blamed 'bad company and drink' for his actions.[98] James Casey, an ex-Connaught Ranger who had deserted from the National Army and was wanted for robbery, died after a 'strenuous fight' with gardaí in Roscommon during April 1924.[99] Other army veterans were convicted of offences varying from fraud to running brothels.[100] Republicans gleefully publicised the numerous cases of Free State personnel's involvement in crime.[101]

There were more colourful, if tragic, examples outside Ireland. James Phelan and Seán McAteer were both union activists and former members of the Irish Citizen Army.

In June 1923 they raided a post office in Scotland Road, the heart of Liverpool's Irish community. In the course of the robbery, Thomas Lovelady, the postmistress' son, was shot dead.[102] Phelan was sentenced to death, but reprieved and remained in jail until 1938. (He subsequently became a renowned author on 'tramp' and prison life.[103]) Local communists were alleged to have helped McAteer escape to the Soviet Union, only for him to die there during the purges in the late 1930s.[104] Even further afield, IRA veteran Hugh Martin was jailed in Australia for a series of violent robberies during 1932. From Derry, Martin had an extensive record of service before the truce and had joined the Free State side in 1922. After emigrating to Australia, he found it hard to find work. Turning to robbery, he earned a reputation as one of the 'coldest, most ruthless men in Australian crime history', narrowly escaping a death sentence for shooting a policeman. Martin was not released until 1947 and jailed again for more minor crimes during the 1950s.[105]

In 1924, 142 armed raids took place in Dublin. However, many banks in the city were now equipped with new Miller electrical alarm equipment and the number of robberies gradually declined.[106] But the countryside remained troubled. In 1924 John Keogh, described as 'a labourer who had turned raparee', was captured in east Galway.[107] The Department of Justice described the 'Keogh gang' as 'well-known Irregulars', and during a spree of house raids and burnings Keogh certainly referred to himself as a 'republican soldier'. He appears to have refused to accept the IRA's ceasefire order, and was more agrarian-radical than criminal.[108] Evidence of responsibility is lacking for many of the other raids that occurred in this period, including some that led to fatalities, such as that of John Doyle during a Dundalk robbery in 1926.[109] In January 1927, Ballinamore, County Leitrim, was the scene of a 'thrilling bank raid'.[110] Up to eight armed men arrived in the town by car in the early hours of the morning, taking over the garda barracks and holding up the occupants. They forced their way into the Ulster Bank but detectives ambushed them inside and a 'regular battle' ensued during which one of the raiders was killed. He was Patrick Crowley, a farmer and blacksmith.[111] The IRA denied Crowley was a volunteer and claimed not to have been involved in bank raids since 1923.[112] While the IRA was responsible for much armed activity, including the assassination of Minister for Justice Kevin O'Higgins in 1927, evidence suggests that as an organisation it eschewed fundraising raids in the period after the Civil War.[113] In 1927 its chief of staff, Maurice Twomey, estimated that £400 a month was required to maintain the organisation. An agreement with the Soviet Union to supply finance from 1925 onwards may have influenced the IRA's decision not to utilise robbery as a form of fundraising. This was accompanied by a significant shift leftwards by the organisation. Yet, while the IRA was supposed to provide military intelligence for the Soviets in return for funds, the arrangement was never very satisfactory.[114] The Great Depression also severely impacted on the ability of republican support networks in the United States to supply cash. In 1934, the IRA complained that it was 'very much in debt' and imposed a £5 weekly levy on its units.[115] Twomey had lamented during 1933 that 'in 1922 we took over the Banks showing that we realised that the people's money was necessary for our freedom. The only mistake was that we did not take enough.' But Twomey's statement reflected a desire for radical social policies more than to raise finance per se.[116]

But some IRA members still engaged in robberies. In February 1926, gardaí uncovered a major arms dump at St Enda's College in Dublin. An IRA inquiry found that a group of its members and ex-members, unemployed and down on their luck, had been planning to use the arms to carry out robberies. But before they could do so one of the group had actually 'sold' the location to gardaí.[117] During 1930 a Dublin Brigade member, Archie Doyle, was expelled after being jailed for taking part in the robbery of £1,609 in wages from a building contractor.[118] (Unknown to his captors and to most of his colleagues, Doyle was one of the men who had killed Kevin O'Higgins.[119]) In April 1929, the Bank of Ireland in Tipperary was robbed of £950. Gardaí arrested three suspects shortly afterwards, two of them, George and James Plant, IRA veterans of some note. During the War of Independence, the Plant family farm near Fethard had been 'extensively used by the IRA as sleeping quarters ... being regarded as comparatively safe from raids owing to its isolated position ... and further owing to the religion of the owners'. (The Plants were Anglican and James had served in the Royal Navy during the First World War.) The brothers had gained reputations as 'courageous and dangerous men' during the Civil War, taking part in bank robberies and firing on gardaí. In 1923 they emigrated to Scotland and from there to North America. While in Chicago they met their accomplice, Patrick Keogh, also an IRA veteran. Gardaí were aware that the Plants had returned to Tipperary in 1929, and that they seemed to have little money and were not seen wearing 'watches, chains, rings etc', the usual symbols of success among returned emigrants.[120] When placed on trial the brothers recognised the court and pleaded guilty, actions expressly forbidden for IRA members. Their lawyer argued that the men were 'sons of a very respectable widowed mother' who had thrown themselves 'heart and soul into the fight for independence in this country'. While he accepted they were guilty, they were 'not the common class of culprit or criminal'. The judge admitted that 'it is shocking to see men like you in the dock' but contended that the men's history made their involvement in crime even worse. He also noted that less than £100 of the stolen cash had been found.[121] As well as recognising the court, the men were not listed as IRA prisoners while in jail and seem to have served their sentences quietly. The gardaí speculated that 'the mother of the Plants is in a very low financial position' and that the missing money may have been used to 'pay off the more pressing, and perhaps all, of her debts'.[122] Their story illustrates some of the features of armed crime in the post-revolutionary era. Men who had experienced combat and life outside the law were sometimes still prepared to utilise their 'skills' in order to gain access to funds. While the 1929 robbery was not carried out for the organisation, George Plant did eventually rejoin the IRA and in 1942 was executed for the murder of a suspected informer, Michael Devereux, in a highly controversial case.[123]

The Ballinamore and Tipperary raids were among the last of that era. Republicans were involved in widespread political activity during the late 1920s, and although the IRA engaged in a variety of armed actions (including shooting gardaí and suspected informers) during that period, even the state did not charge them with involvement in robberies. It would take almost a decade of political realignment and organisational fissures before the IRA would return to this tactic.

Chapter 3

Rethinking and Re-organisation: From the 1930s to the Northern War

THE 1930s MARKED a crucial period in the IRA's political history. In late 1931, the Cumann na nGaedheal government introduced the most stringent security legislation since the Civil War. The Public Safety Act provided for military courts, non-jury trials and bans on the republican (and socialist) press.[1] The government claimed that the laws were necessary because of increasing IRA violence and the threat posed by the 'communist' nature of the republican political programme. Though the IRA was shaken by these new laws, it weathered the storm, in part because the measures were opposed by the Fianna Fáil party and seen by many as a transparent attempt by an unpopular government to use a 'red scare' to remain in power. The IRA gave political and practical support to Fianna Fáil in the 1932 general election, which saw that party come to power for the first time. It did so again in the 1933 election in which Fianna Fáil won an overall majority. De Valera's government released IRA prisoners and the new political atmosphere saw the organisation recruit widely.[2] The honeymoon, however, was short-lived. The IRA was soon engaged in widespread conflict with supporters of the new Fine Gael party, often organised as part of the fascist Blueshirt movement. Continuing armed activities led to republicans being jailed under the security legislation introduced in 1931, while IRA criticism of the government led to a widening chasm with Fianna Fáil. Internal disputes between left and right within the IRA caused a split and the formation of the socialist Republican Congress in 1934. From then on, the IRA faced a decline in membership, increasingly antagonistic relations with state forces and political marginalisation. De Valera's government now framed condemnations of the 'new IRA' in terms of the organisation's lack of continuity with the 1919–23 period. Indeed, a number of anti-treaty IRA veterans were actually recruited into the garda detective branch during this time.[3] In 1935, de Valera likened IRA intervention during a strike to the actions of a 'racketeering organisation'.[4] Between 1936 and 1939, the Fianna Fáil government introduced significant new security legislation, particularly the Offences Against the State Act (1939) which definitively placed the IRA, as a subversive organisation, outside the law.[5] It was outlawed and leading members, such as Twomey, jailed.

During this period, the IRA had briefly resumed a crime-fighting role – albeit in very different circumstances to those that prevailed in the early 1920s – when it clashed with the so-called 'animal gangs' in Dublin. These were groups of young men from Dublin's inner city, who gained a fearsome reputation for using weapons in feuds, and engaging in 'mercenary money-lending or outright extortion of shop-owners'. Some accounts of the 1930s also stressed their role in reactionary violence, with the 'animal gang' a 'one size fits all' label applied to those involved in attacks on the left.[6] The gangs originated among teenagers, so-called 'newsboys', who sold newspapers on the streets. In the autumn of 1934, Dublin newspaper production was halted by a strike. The IRA's *An Phoblacht* was the only paper allowed to continue publication by the strike committee and was sold by newsboys as usual. However, the sellers demanded a cheaper rate for the paper and when this was refused, clashes ensued. Several IRA members were hospitalised and the windows of the *An Phoblacht* offices broken by gang members.[7] A parade by republicans carrying sticks failed to dissuade the youths from further confrontation. Ultimately, armed IRA members raided locations associated with the newsboys, such the Ardee Hall in Talbot Street, and threatened those they found there. *An Phoblacht* claimed that the 'Dublin Brigade' was about to 'clean up city gangs'.[8] But tension between republicans and the gangs continued for some years afterwards. The IRA had to provide armed escorts for their members returning from parades because of trouble with gang members, who tried to steal their weapons.[9] In February 1938, a youth named William O'Brien was shot dead by IRA volunteer Eddie Whelan after one such confrontation.[10] While the IRA had couched their opposition to the gangs in the language of policing, at least part of the conflict was about hegemony on Dublin's streets. There was also undoubtedly a connection between some gang members and the IRA's enemies on the right.[11]

By then, the IRA was on a new course. Under the leadership of Seán Russell and with the promise of funding from Irish-American supporters, it had decided to embark upon a bombing campaign in Britain. The results were disastrous. Once the Second World War began, de Valera's government moved harshly against the IRA, seeing it, and its clandestine contacts with Germany, as a threat to neutrality. Internment, hunger strikes and executions followed, on both sides of the border.[12] Republicans were increasingly isolated, with external sources of funding (from both the US and Germany) drying up.[13] Gardaí had suspected Belfast IRA members of the robbery of £1,931 from a bank messenger in Dublin's O'Connell Street in June 1936. However, it was in 1940 that the IRA leadership authorised such tactics for the first time since the Civil War.[14] On 20 September, banks and post offices on Belfast's Falls Road were raided by armed men – £2,165 was stolen and gun battles with pursuing police saw an IRA man and an RUC officer wounded.[15] During November, IRA suspects in Dublin were found to have plans of city banks in their possession.[16] This forced the cancellation of several planned raids. In early 1941, there was a series of small robberies of Dublin moneylenders, loan offices and shops. Gardaí suspected that the raids may not have been 'official IRA jobs' but carried out by republicans 'deported from England and who were destitute'.[17] Indeed, two Dublin bank raids in 1940 had been carried out by Robert Murphy, a union official, who, though a 1916 veteran, had no connection to the contemporary IRA. Murphy, whose wife and baby were seriously ill, was desperate for cash. Jailed for five years, he also lost his military service pension.[18]

Dundalk post office was raided by the IRA during April 1941 and a clerk wounded while £940 was taken.[19] A month later the Northern Bank at Oldcastle, County Meath, was robbed of £704. One IRA member, James Clarke, was captured and sentenced to two years and twelve strokes of the 'cat' for his involvement in the raid, while another suspect, Patrick Dermody, was shot dead by detectives a year later. In June 1941, £636 was taken from a bank at Castlepollard. The chief suspect was

Dundalk IRA man Richard Goss, who was captured after a shoot-out in July 1942 and subsequently executed.[20] Another series of Dublin raids was foiled when gardaí seized plans for a number of the city's post offices from IRA members that winter. But in Belfast in January 1942, armed men robbed the senior pay clerk of the Air Raid Protection Service and took £4,800. In the melee the clerk was wounded, as was one of the raiders, an incident thought to be the inspiration for F.L. Green's novel *Odd Man Out*.[21] In February the IRA's chief of staff, Seán Harrington, was arrested in Dublin with cash from the Belfast robbery. Over the next two years there were small-scale robberies of rent offices, bookmakers and pawnbrokers. Raiders also targeted Dublin's Jewish Club and a number of the city's moneylenders, some of whom were also Jewish.[22] A search for easy targets rather than any ethnic animus seems to have been the motivation. Not all such activities were authorised by the IRA. In April 1943 Patrick McElroy and Joseph Haines were arrested during an attempted robbery of a railway paymaster in Dublin. Both men were veterans of the International Brigades in the Spanish Civil War. McElroy, who had been wounded in Spain and was unemployed, explained that he 'decided he would get enough money to give him a start. The "job" appeared so simple that he took the chance.' While Haines, who had tried to dissuade his comrade, was acquitted, McElroy was sentenced to seven years in jail.[23] Exceptions to the generally minor robberies were a bank raid in Strabane in February 1943 in which £1,500 was taken and the robbery of £4,455 from a wages van at the Player Wills factory in Dublin in July. The gang who carried out the Dublin raid was reputed to include Archie Doyle (despite his having been expelled from the IRA for another robbery in 1930) and Jackie Griffith. Griffith was shot dead by detectives a week later while cycling down Holles Street. Reeling from arrests and internal dissension, the IRA did not carry out any major robberies after that, though small raids continued.

J. Bowyer Bell described how, because of the robberies, 'the image of the IRA as an Army of the pure had been tarnished. Many decent people now felt they were little more than a Celtic branch of the Chicago gangsters'.[24] In fact the robberies were a consequence of the IRA's political isolation, not its cause, but they certainly further marginalised the organisation. As a result, when the movement attempted to regroup in the late 1940s, it was decided to avoid such activities at all costs. The post-war IRA leadership declared that it would steer clear of 'any type of aggressive military action', including robberies in the republic. Instead, all energies would be focused on a campaign north of the border.[25] This ruling was formalised as General Order No. 8 in 1954. The IRA adhered to this throughout its border campaign from 1956 to 1962.

The failure of that campaign led the IRA to another period of re-thinking and reorganisation. As a movement made up of what the Department of Justice described as 'nondescript persons in lower middle-class and working-class families', funds were never plentiful.[26] During 1965, IRA leaders drew up a very ambitious plan for political and military expansion, but realised that this would require far more funds than the organisation possessed.[27]

Part of the rethinking involved a cautious move leftwards, partly inspired by the IRA's own history during the 1930s and also by the global landscape during the 1960s. A belief that funding could be sought from abroad was also a factor. Indeed, there were optimistic approaches to the Chinese government but these yielded nothing.[28] So, in the mid-1960s senior IRA members once again discussed the possibility of money raids.[29] The movement's chief of staff, Cathal Goulding, ruled out such activities, recalling that the IRA had 'lost a tremendous amount of popular support' as a result of engaging in robberies during the 1940s.[30] Nevertheless, the gardaí believed that the IRA leadership had given approval for hold-ups in Northern Ireland (therefore not contravening Army Order No. 8). Northern units were supposed to submit particulars to the chief of staff for approval. In October 1965, £1,300 was stolen from the car of a Belfast bookmaker and £1,000 sent to IRA headquarters in Dublin and the balance retained for the Belfast organisation.[31]

In August 1967, IRA officers met in Tipperary to discuss their organisation's future. Among the items on the agenda was fundraising. As the meeting's minutes made clear, money was scarce:

... in March of 1966 the Army had a balance of £770 which was added to by a £100 in subs. and by £395 in Sweep money. The concert tour was a failure to the tume [*sic*] of £500. The present situation was that the Army owed it's [*sic*] staff members £273 and £334 to individuals.[32]

During the debates that followed several delegates echoed the view of an Armagh officer that 'money was the chief problem [and] we should be prepared to take it where we can get it'. It was noted, however, that any publicity surrounding IRA men captured on fundraising operations might be embarrassing. A Tyrone officer felt that 'money should be taken' and that the 'Army should accept responsibility' for volunteers captured during these raids. Army council member Malachy McGurran believed that 'money should be taken where possible as he could not see any other way of providing money in the amounts we would need'. However, Limerick officer Paddy Mulcahy opposed this as he thought such tactics had 'got us a bad name before'.[33] There was no concrete decision reached on the matter, but legal fundraising methods were unlikely to fulfil the IRA's needs. A tour by Cathal Goulding to the US in late 1968 yielded just £865.[34] At its convention that year, the IRA agreed that 'contact be made with international Socialist revolutionary underground groups and Socialist Governments anywhere, to investigate the possibility of obtaining arms and finance unconditionally'.[35] Yet in the absence of such aid, other republicans had already shown the apparent value of alternative methods.

In December 1965 a Dublin rent office was raided for cash. One of the raiders, Joe Dillon, an IRA member unhappy with the organisation's lack of military activity, was sentenced to five years in jail.[36] Afterwards, disgruntled IRA volunteers and republican veterans associated with far-left politics began to coalesce. In January 1967 this grouping robbed the home of a Dublin arms dealer.[37] They then took £3,500 in a raid on the Royal Bank in

Drumcondra a month later.[38] This was the first major bank robbery in the south since the 1940s. During April and June 1968, the group robbed three banks of a total of £8,300.[39] In Newry in early March 1969 they took £12,000 in a bank raid during which shots were fired at the RUC.[40] On 15 August 1969 they stole £800 in a raid in Baltinglass. The following month £8,000 was taken from banks in Dublin and Kells, with the raids claimed in the name of the 'Saor Éire Action Group'.[41] In early 1970 a spokesman explained that the group was 'attempting to act as a fuse or detonator to the Irish revolutionary struggle'. He claimed that the 'money expropriated from the banks is used to purchase arms and equipment for the forthcoming struggle'.[42] But there were those who saw Saor Éire as 'a group of cowboys who believed the path to national liberation lay in robbing banks'.[43] Indeed, the organisation had already attracted members of Dublin's criminal milieu, such as Christy Dunne.[44] In February 1970, Saor Éire carried out a robbery in Rathdrum, County Wicklow, during which armed men in battle dress set up roadblocks, cut telephone wires and effectively took over the town. In early April, during an attempted bank raid on Dublin's Arran Quay, an unarmed garda, Richard Fallon, was shot dead. This was the first killing of a garda by republicans since 1942 and it caused outrage.[45] One activist remembered 'sitting in a pub in Dún Laoghaire as the news came in' and hearing 'working men at the bar railing angrily against the IRA'.[46] The IRA itself quickly denied any involvement and criticised the perpetrators for making repressive legislation more likely.[47] A major hunt was launched for the raiders and the names of seven suspects published in the national press.[48] Nevertheless, Saor Éire continued to carry out robberies, although with most of its members on the run it was already splintering.[49]

But in fact the IRA leadership had already begun to emulate the dissidents. On 14 May 1969 the organisation had robbed a Securicor delivery van at Dublin Airport, taking £24,600. At first, the authorities were reported to be baffled by what *The Irish Times* called the 'complexity and ingenuity' of the robbery.[50] Cathal Goulding denied IRA responsibility and suggested a 'splinter' group might be involved. Within weeks, however, the gardaí recovered £18,000, while two IRA members were eventually jailed.[51] The Department of Justice knew that what it called the 'commando-style operation' had been carried out by the IRA and claimed that 'further armed raids for large sums of money have been abandoned owing to preventive police action but it is known that the organisation is very short of money and it is likely that they will try again'.[52] Try again they would, but after August 1969 in very different circumstances.

That month, inter-communal violence in Belfast saw seven people killed and hundreds injured. British troops were sent onto the streets and by December the IRA split into what became rival Official (OIRA) and Provisional (PIRA) organisations. Both claimed to be 'the' IRA but the Provisionals emphasised the need to engage the British militarily in order to force them from Ireland, while the Officials put more stress on social agitation. Significantly, however, both would utilise armed robbery to fund themselves. Between 1967 and 1972, £107,570 was stolen in bank robberies in the republic, the numbers of which escalated after 1970.[53] Between 1969 and 1970, there had been just seventeen such robberies. In 1971, there were thirty, but in 1972 this number rose to 132. The garda commissioner was in no doubt that 'the increase in the number of robberies [was] in great measure ... due to the conditions obtaining in the Six County area and their influence on criminal behaviour here'.[54] On occasion people carrying out the robberies even told bank customers the funds were intended 'for the North'.[55] However, unlike Saor Éire, neither IRA publicly claimed responsibility for these raids and often denied involvement in them.[56]

An indication of the difference armed raids could make to paramilitary finances is illustrated by a discussion that took place at the October 1972 Official IRA convention. The organisation's director of operations, Seamus Costello, outlined how since 1971 there had been 'a total income of £92,000 ... £70,000 came as a direct result of operations and £22,000 from USA, etc'. Of this total income, '£22,378 was spent on weapons and the QM's [quartermaster's] department'. This was quite a difference compared to 1967, when the organisation was £600 in debt. Costello, however, was already warning of the need to diversify, stating that 'we should not continue to depend solely on ops [operations] for income for reasons of the effort in time and manpower and the risk element'. He suggested instead the imposition of a levy of £1,000 per month from the combined foreign support organisations.[57] The OIRA had declared a conditional ceasefire in May 1972 but fundraising operations had continued, as had other forms of armed activity. Among the dangers for all organisations was that such activities could become an attraction in themselves. During 1972 disgruntled OIRA activists in south Down had complained that:

> ... one unit is known widely in the area as a gang of criminals. Money liberated for the army from the control of capitalist banks was not passed on but was misappropriated ... this unit ... is now operating a racket in stolen cars ... working men's property has in many cases been stolen ... Radios from cars, goods from shops, cars have been stolen and burned when the only reason for taking them seems to be a desire not to walk home from the pub at all costs.[58]

By the mid-1970s, the OIRA had become adept at fraud centred around the construction industry. The UK Inland Revenue allowed building contractors to settle their tax affairs at the conclusion of the year. Rather than pay tax on a weekly basis, the subcontractors were granted tax exemption certificates, which enabled the main contractor to pay in gross without income tax being deducted. If false certificates were produced, then contractors could present a figure to the authorities and pay a percentage to the OIRA. With major building work starting to take place in areas of Belfast, such as the Lower Falls, where the Officials were strong, the tax exemption racket rapidly became a source of funding for them.[59] The Officials also set up legal construction companies and established social clubs, which could be used to launder money. Other paramilitary groups followed suit. By 1976, the Northern Ireland Office was aware that the Provisionals, Officials and the loyalist groups were running construction companies.[60]

The Official IRA continued to carry out armed robberies but after their ceasefire they placed great importance on developing a political base, particularly in the republic. In 1977, the Officials renamed their political wing Sinn Féin – The Workers' Party and denied any connection with paramilitary activity. A discussion by the OIRA leadership that year heard an admission that 'we as a political organisation ... have suffered defeats because of our association with violence and illegality'. But it was agreed there was still a 'need and a role for the IRA' because 'without a body of armed members we would not be able to survive'. One suggestion was to 'publicly disband the IRA, then reorganise secretly and with more care regarding membership'. This, however, might result in a loss of support as 'we would be bound to have IRA members who would not or could not understand the motive'. Instead, activities such as robberies would be increasingly handled by activists who were not connected publicly to the political organisation.[61] As one leading figure explained, 'nobody, I hope, will deny the need for us to have fundraising units. If we accept this then we must recognise that at some point in time something may go wrong with dire consequences for all. This is one reason why we need capable but unknown people engaged in this activity.' This messy compromise meant that the Official IRA was not publicly stood down, but its existence was now denied. Internally it was usually referred to as 'Group B' and many ordinary members of Sinn Féin – The Workers' Party would be either ignorant or only vaguely aware of its activities. But, inevitably, questions continued to be asked about what had happened to the Official IRA. In 1982, Tomás Mac Giolla, president of what was now The Workers' Party, told RTÉ radio that 'there was no reason to think that it [the OIRA] still exists'.[62] The OIRA leadership was, it seems, also quite clear that lying, publicly and internally, was a necessity.

Such ruses, however, were not always successful. In April 1977, a Securicor van in County Derry was robbed of £229,977, the largest amount stolen in a robbery in Northern Ireland to that date. Despite careful planning, the raiders were spotted by police and arrested. At their trial in December, it was revealed that the heist had been carried out by an Official IRA unit.[63] In September 1978, Group B members carried out a robbery outside Cork city. A female clerk was wounded during the raid, in which £10,350 was stolen. After a brief gun battle with gardaí the raiders surrendered.[64] Five men were arrested.[65] The prosecution opposed bail because of the men's paramilitary backgrounds. Their membership of the Official IRA was mentioned at the trial but the defendants' orders were clear: they told their lawyer that the robbery had been solely for themselves and disavowed any connection with the OIRA.[66] While awaiting trial they were not allowed to associate with their OIRA comrades in Portlaoise Prison and were given none of the privileges available to paramilitary inmates. The OIRA prison commander went through the motions of refusing to have anything to do with the men. It was not until sentences of twelve years were imposed, by which stage publicity had died down and political damage had been minimised, that the men were allowed to join their comrades. By the 1980s, Official IRA members who were jailed served their sentences as 'ordinary' prisoners. This marked a significant departure from the traditional importance of republican prisoners being recognised as such and reflected the belief of senior OIRA leaders such as Seán Garland that these practices were no longer useful for a revolutionary organisation. It also meant that the organisation could avoid association with, and justify opposition to, demands by the Provisionals for political status, on the basis that this was 'elitist' because all inmates were victims of a 'corrupt' system.[67]

By the late 1980s, counterfeiting including the distribution of fake dollars, allegedly produced in North Korea, had become part of Group B's remit.[68] (The evolution from armed heists to international espionage is vividly illustrated in fictional form in the online novel *Superdollar*.[69]) A British government briefing document suggested that the OIRA was 'arguably the first Irish terrorist organisation to go over – even if temporarily – almost fully to what is understood as organised crime'.[70] Despite such subterfuge, involvement in these 'special activities' carried major risks, among them periodic media exposure.[71] The failure to secure major foreign financial aid meant, however, that they remained necessary. A way to minimise political embarrassment was to cooperate with 'ordinary' criminals. There had been informal connections between criminals and the Official IRA in Dublin since the early 1970s. This was how Eamon Kelly, from Dublin's north inner city, first entered into the orbit of the OIRA. Plans for robberies were shared, or weapons 'rented' out, in exchange for a share of the profits. But allegations about criminality and occasional exposures by hostile media helped produce a crisis that led to the split in The Workers' Party in 1992.[72]

The group using the Saor Éire title had continued operations into the early 1970s and both the OIRA and the Provisionals were wary of the smaller faction's recklessness. Saor Éire's provocative activities almost led to the introduction of internment in late 1970, after which the Provisional IRA threatened to take action against them. The Provisional's leader Seán Mac Stíofáin claimed that he had sent a message to Saor Éire that if they were 'responsible for internment down here you're all dead'.[73] Any remaining romance around the group disappeared in October 1971 when Peter Graham, a young left-winger who had joined them, was murdered. He had been beaten and shot by Saor Éire members seeking information about money and weapons.[74] By then the group had been completely overshadowed by the escalating crisis in Northern Ireland. In May 1973 Saor Éire prisoners in Portlaoise prison severed connections with the organisation, claiming that 'undesirable elements have been able to operate around its fringe and carry out actions' under its name.[75]

It is difficult to assess which organisation was responsible for the majority of armed crime in the early years of the Northern Ireland conflict. The violence after 1970, with almost 500 people killed during 1972 alone, meant that very few people paid any attention to often small-scale robberies. All paramilitary groups, republican and loyalist, carried them out, but opportunists and increasingly criminals attracted by the ease of armed robbery did so as well. In fact the biggest robbery in the republic until that date was the taking of £67,000 from the Allied Irish Bank in Dublin's Grafton Street in October 1972.[76] The gang involved were led by two English criminals, the Littlejohn brothers, Keith and Kenneth, who had associated with Official IRA members but later claimed to be working for British intelligence, carrying out raids to discredit republicans.[77] If the Officials had been early trailblazers, the Provisionals and others soon caught up.[78] Initially, the Provisional IRA had formally eschewed robberies in the south, with Sinn Féin president Ruairí Ó Brádaigh claiming such activities were 'completely contrary to the national interest ... this is not the time and the 26 counties is not the place'.[79] However, in the same period four young Belfast Provos had been charged with an armed robbery in Omeath, County Louth, suggesting that not all volunteers were paying attention to these orders.[80] Robberies in Britain *were* authorised, with the proviso that volunteers captured on such missions would not be claimed as IRA members.[81] Fundraising operations in the six counties were also permitted, and Provisional lore has it that Dolours and Marian Price held up a branch of the Allied Irish Bank in Belfast disguised as 'fresh-faced nuns'.[82] Eventually, the organisation's policy on raids in the republic was adjusted.[83] During 1974, the Provisional IRA robbed Tralee's General Post Office, netting £74,000, and the Chase Manhattan Bank in Shannon, taking £159,000.[84] Another notable IRA heist was the robbery of £24,000 in gate receipts from the Munster hurling final at Thurles in July 1977.[85]

Republicans were correct in worrying that armed activity in the south could lead to a clampdown on their activities, as their actions contributed to the introduction of a new range of special powers between 1972 and 1976. These included a non-jury Special Criminal Court, an amendment to the Offences Against the State Act (OASA) which shifted the 'burden of proof onto the defendant' and meant that a suspect could 'be convicted by a judge on the say-so of a senior police officer', and media censorship.[86] Between 1972 and 1980 there were 8,105 arrests under Section 30 of the OASA; 1,545 people were charged.[87] Despite worries about civil liberties, with concerns that the gardaí were operating a 'heavy gang' in order to secure convictions, the measures were justified by the government on the basis that the state itself was under threat from a 'cohesive set of determined criminals'.[88] Between 1974 and 1976 there were eighty-one armed bank raids and fifty-six post office robberies in the republic.[89] From July to December 1976 there were forty-one major robberies in the state, with over £200,000 stolen.[90] Not all were carried out by republicans.[91] Two Belfast men were jailed in Dublin for a string of armed robberies during 1976, in which £27,000 was taken. The duo had actually been forced to leave Belfast by the IRA after being accused of criminal activities.[92] In other cases, such as the October 1978 robbery of a post office in Donegal town, in which £225,000 was netted, it is highly unlikely anyone but the IRA could have been responsible. Heavily armed men took over the local garda station, smashed communications equipment and stole files, before raiding the post office and making off with the loot.[93] By that year, some police and legal sources in Dublin would assert that while the major raids were carried out by republicans, perhaps just '30 per cent of robberies are political'.[94] Moreover, gardaí were aware of the danger of concentrating on 'subversive' activity while 'ordinary' crime escalated.[95] But as one lawyer explained, 'the majority of the non-political robbers here … have been introduced to armed robberies by the example of the Northern para-militaries'.[96] As most gardaí remained unarmed, soldiers were increasingly used as back-up, leading one commentator to reflect during 1979 that 'more precautions [and] more armed men were needed to convey money from place to place in Ireland than ever were necessary to ferry gold dust from camp to railroad in the American West'.[97]

By the mid-1970s another armed organisation, formed after a split with the Officials, had emerged on the scene. The Irish National Liberation Army (INLA) was associated with the Irish Republican Socialist Party (IRSP) founded in December 1974. It too faced the problem of funding itself, and from an early stage its supporters were being jailed for involvement in robberies.[98] In March 1976 four IRSP members were charged with the robbery of £200,000 from a mail train in County Kildare. Despite evidence of garda brutality in forcing their confessions, the four were convicted in the Special Criminal Court and sentenced to lengthy prison terms.[99] Unusually, the Provisional IRA claimed in 1980 that they, and not the INLA, had carried out that train robbery.[100] But one of the biggest robberies during 1978 *was* carried out by the INLA, when a Brink's-Mat security van was held up at Barna Gap in County Limerick and £460,000 taken.[101] (The IRA publicly expressed regret that they had not carried out the Barna Gap heist.[102])

One of the risks of armed robbery for paramilitary groups was the temptation for those involved to keep some of the takings for themselves, or to simply carry out their own 'jobs'. IRA volunteers were paid a wage, one recalling that in the early 1970s they were 'given an allowance of £8 a week for socialising, at the time a fiver would have got you a good night out'.[103] However, those with families and other responsibilities could face financial difficulties. Belfast IRA member Richard O'Rawe explained how he and

another Volunteer ... had gotten drunk in Kelly's bar, and when we ran out of money we decided to do a 'homer', which is an IRA euphemism for a self-gain robbery. We borrowed a sympathiser's vehicle, one that most Volunteers in our Battalion knew to have been used regularly by the Ballymurphy Volunteers, and drove down the Falls Road. We robbed the first place that caught our eye. We were unmasked while doing the robbery and, while the RUC was not informed of our robbery, the IRA was. Within a couple of hours it had traced the vehicle and identified us ... we got less than fifty pounds from the robbery and we blew it on drink that night.[104]

O'Rawe and his friend were kneecapped and drummed out of the IRA for their escapade. O'Rawe later rejoined and was jailed for another (sanctioned) robbery, becoming a senior member of the IRA's prison staff during the H-Block protest. 'Homers' were a recurring problem for all of the armed republican organisations. Punishments varied but could be far harsher than that meted out to O'Rawe and his comrade. In February 1979, Donegal IRA member Patrick Sills died after being beaten and shot because of his involvement in an unofficial armed raid.[105]

By the mid-1970s the assertion that republicans were motivated by criminality was used by the British government to deny political status to those jailed as a result of the conflict. The research of Belfast-based academics Kevin Boyle, Tom Hadden and Paddy Hillyard found that most IRA activists, at least, had no connection with crime before becoming involved in armed activity. They were 'satisfied that the data establishes beyond reasonable doubt that the bulk of Republican offenders are young men and women without criminal records in the ordinary sense'. While 'some may have been involved in public disorders of the kind which frequently take place in the areas in which they live', they were 'not, as is sometimes implied by government ministers or the press, habitual criminals or in some way psychologically disturbed. Most are broadly representative of the communities from which they come.'[106] In 1978 a leaked British intelligence document was seized on by republicans as proof of the falsity of the accusations of criminality. The report stated that the 'evidence of the calibre of rank and file terrorists does not support the view that they are merely mindless hooligans drawn from the unemployed and un-employable', and that the IRA 'trains and uses its members with some care'. The Provisional IRA was 'essentially a working class organisation based in the ghetto areas of the cities and in the poorer rural areas. Thus if members of the middle class and graduates become more deeply involved they have to forfeit their life style.' At leadership level there was 'a strata of intelligent, astute and experienced terrorists who provide the backbone of the organisation'. The report concluded that the violence was 'likely to continue while the British remain in Northern Ireland'.

What was also significant was its assessment of how the IRA was funded. It argued that

armed robbery within Ireland is almost certainly the greatest source of income for the IRA. In the North since 1971 thefts have been running at some £500,000 per year. In the South up to 1976 the annual loss was about £700,000 but in 1977 it was over £900,000 ... the proceeds of the theft of readily marketable goods also sometimes go to the Provisionals. We estimate that income from theft is running at at least £550,000 a year.

It also suggested that other forms of fundraising were exploited, with 'the main continuing forms of racketeering' being 'protection payments from shops and businesses, and fraud involving dole money and "lost" pension books. We estimate that the annual income through this is about £250,000.' Republicans would have disputed many of these claims. But waging an armed campaign, with limited funds from abroad, made such activities attractive and perhaps inevitable. While the media often sensationalised Irish-American sympathy for the IRA, the British estimated that NORAID, the main republican support group in the US, was providing funds of less than $100,000 a year.[107] Other republicans estimate that money from the US constituted at most only 10–20 per cent of the IRA's annual budget.[108]

But there were other costs from involvement in such activities. Between 1970 and 1980 five gardaí and four civilians were killed as a result of robberies by republicans in the south. Placed against the death toll north of the border, these figures are low.[109] But in a society that had seen almost no armed crime until the 1970s and where deadly violence against the police was rare, these killings were particularly shocking. In August 1973, the Provisional IRA shot dead 54-year-old James Farrell during a wages robbery in Dublin.[110] In August 1974, wages clerk Jerome O'Connor was shot and killed during a robbery by Official IRA members in Galway.[111] In September 1975, off-duty garda Michael Reynolds was killed while tackling bank raiders in Dublin.[112] In December 1976, a detective was shot and critically wounded by IRA members during a robbery at Cornelscourt in Dublin.[113] In February 1978, Provisional IRA members fatally wounded 51-year-old Bernard Browne during the robbery of a supermarket in Donegal.[114] In August 1979, 32-year-old Eamon Ryan was shot dead when he entered a bank during a robbery by the Provisional IRA in Tramore.[115] In July 1980, Detective John Morley and Garda Henry Byrne were killed in a gun battle after a robbery in County Roscommon. In October that year, Detective Seamus Quaid was killed in a struggle with an IRA member while conducting follow-up searches after another bank raid.[116] In the popular mind these events were seen as evidence that 'the Northern troubles ... have spilled over with a vengeance'.[117] There had been a recent series of robberies for which Provisional IRA members were charged throughout the period, during which, though nobody was killed, shots had been fired at unarmed gardaí. In several cases, such as that of Eamon Ryan, who was with his young son when shot, the killings seemed callous. The trial following Bernard Browne's killing 'reflected poorly on republicans, not alone for the death of the shopkeeper but also in terms of exploiting and pressurising young people to join the IRA'.[118] John Morley and Seamus Quaid were well-known GAA personalities as well as garda officers.[119] In addition to causing resentment against the organisations concerned, the killings helped solidify the image of the perpetrators as criminals. In the aftermath of the Quaid shooting *The Irish Press*, the most nationalist of the daily newspapers, feared 'something evil and even uncontrollable' was being unleashed by the 'terrible cancer of Northern Ireland'. Gerry Collins, the Fianna Fáil minister for justice, warned that people were 'fed up to the hilt ... with the way armed criminals, in particular the subversives, the Provisional people, are carrying out a campaign of armed robbery on banks, payrolls and post offices'.[120] Though republicans were certainly aware of the need to avoid conflict in the south, their fundraising needs helped create a situation where the political consensus supported the maintenance of draconian legislation.[121] In reality, however, while killings associated with republicans contributed to the increase in homicides in the Republic of Ireland after 1970, these were always a minority of cases; most murders had no connection to politics.[122]

Despite a revival in political support during the 1981 H-Block hunger strikes, the republican need for funding remained critical. The electoral successes of Sinn Féin and the growing professionalism of its political work intensified this demand.[123] To replenish their funds, the Provisionals adopted what was a relatively new tactic for them: kidnapping.[124] In October 1981, the supermarket owner Ben Dunne was abducted in Armagh. He was held for a week before being released, and though officially denied, it was claimed that a ransom of £300,000 had been paid.[125] In February 1983, the champion racehorse Shergar was stolen from a stud farm in Kildare. It is thought that the animal became uncontrollable and was put down.[126] The disappearance of the horse was a sensation, and it was believed the IRA was responsible. The organisation's involvement in kidnappings came to light in dramatic fashion later that year. During August four IRA members were badly wounded by detectives near the home of tycoon Galen Weston at Roundwood, County Wicklow. It was alleged they had arrived with the intention of abducting the businessman.[127] In November 1983, the IRA kidnapped supermarket executive Don Tidey in Dublin. For three weeks there was an intense manhunt across the state. Tidey was finally rescued in a wood near Ballinamore, County Leitrim, in December. During his rescue there was a confused gun battle in which 22-year-old trainee garda Gary Sheehan and a soldier, Private Patrick Kelly, were killed. The deaths of the garda and soldier were disastrous for the image of the republican movement. Its response was to argue that the 'attempted massacre of IRA Volunteers at Roundwood' was 'obviously in the minds of the Volunteers who opened fire in self-defence at Free State forces at Ballinamore'. The IRA justified kidnapping as its 'struggle is being fought against tremendous odds [and] because of the disastrous, immoral failure of Free State governments to face up to their responsibility and use their resources to end the evil of British rule in the North of Ireland'.[128] Ultimately, however, it was dropped as a fundraising tactic.

The Provisionals would never abandon armed robbery and the inevitable consequences continued to haunt them and other republican groups. In February 1982 an unarmed, uniformed garda, Patrick Reynolds, was killed in Dublin by an INLA faction which had just carried out a major bank robbery.[129] In August 1984, a garda detective, Frank Hand, was shot dead during an IRA raid on a post office in Meath.[130] Garda sergeant Patrick Morrissey was killed by INLA members after a robbery in Ardee, County Louth, in June 1985. The unarmed Morrissey had been wounded and then shot again at close range while he lay on the ground.[131] The death of a policeman in such circumstances arguably contributed to a lack of public scrutiny when the police used force themselves. In November 1987, Martin Bryan, an associate of Dessie O'Hare, was shot dead and O'Hare himself critically wounded at a roadblock manned by gardaí and soldiers in County Kilkenny.[132] Seven months later, IRA member Hugh Hehir was killed by detectives after another post office robbery in Feakle, County Clare.[133] The willingness of the gardaí to use deadly force and the reluctance to question this was apparent after a bank raid in Athy, County Kildare, in January 1990. Nine people were shot, one fatally, in what was initially reported as a major gun battle between detectives and raiders.[134] It soon transpired that the dead man, Dublin criminal Austin Higgins, and those wounded, who included bank staff, gardaí and a passer-by, had *all* been hit by garda fire; the raiders had not used their weapons at all.[135] While a British Tory MP mischievously demanded an inquiry and contrasted it with the Irish government's criticism of the police north of the border, there was little public outrage.[136] Indeed, one opinion poll found that 95 per cent of respondents agreed that the gardaí had been right to open fire.[137] Just five months later two more bank robbers were shot dead by detectives in Dublin.[138]

Despite these risks and the provision of huge supplies of weapons and finance by the Libyan regime from the mid-1980s, the IRA continued to carry out robberies.[139] In January 1992, the biggest single robbery in the state's history was carried out by the Provos in Waterford, when £2.1 million was taken from the Allied Irish Bank at Lisduggan.[140] But engaging in such activities could also impact on Sinn Féin's political ambitions. In May 1990, shots were fired when gardaí intercepted an IRA unit as it prepared to rob a bank in Enniscorthy, County Wexford. One of those arrested had been a Sinn Féin election candidate.[141] Such negative publicity hindered efforts to be taken seriously as a political force. Talks during the early stages of the peace process were disrupted by the IRA killing of postal worker Frank Kerr during a robbery in Newry in November 1994.[142] The shooting dead of Detective Jerry McCabe during a robbery in County Limerick in June 1996 had reverberations for Sinn Féin, particularly in the Limerick area, for several years afterwards.[143] Despite a realisation that other forms of fundraising, such as running drinking clubs, were less risky, the problem for the IRA, as one activist explained, was that 'the advantage of a bank robbery is that it's over and done with immediately and the movement gets what it needs'. Establishing front businesses like pubs meant interaction with the Revenue Commissioners and other state bodies, creating complications which successful robberies did not.[144] The war in Northern Ireland after 1970 transformed the image of the IRA in a variety of ways. But one of these, though unwelcome to republicans, was the popular association of the movement with crime. In the early stages of the conflict it had sought to minimise potential damage by limiting such activities to the 'war zone' but after 1973 a key part of the IRA's remit, especially in the south, involved armed robberies and other forms of illegal fundraising.

Chapter 4

Blurring of Boundaries?

FTER CONFLICT ERUPTED in Northern Ireland, republicans became involved in policing certain varieties of crime.[1] Criminals were beaten up, tarred and feathered or tied to lampposts with placards outlining their crimes. Others were ordered to leave the north, on pain of being shot if they returned. But the most common form of punishment was kneecapping – the shooting of a victim in the kneecap (or occasionally knees and elbows), the bullet smashing the bone and severing veins and arteries. The RUC began to register such shootings in 1973, but they had been occurring since 1970 in both nationalist and loyalist districts.[2] Republicans carried out an estimated 1,228 punishment shootings between 1973 and 1997, though almost certainly many more went unreported.[3] If done with precision and with low-velocity weapons, on the thigh or lower leg, the wounds would be painful but often superficial. Indeed, punishment beatings with baseball bats or other implements could actually cause more severe damage.[4] Yet, in some cases, either through carelessness or deliberately when rifles or even shotguns were used, victims were maimed or lost limbs. Nevertheless, despite hundreds of such shootings, it was not until 1982 that the first fatality from a Provisional IRA kneecapping occurred. Derryman Colm Carey, accused of involvement in 'persistent criminality', was shot with a rifle and bled to death. The IRA expressed 'regret' at his death and promised an 'urgent inquiry'.[5] But despite often brutal results, there could be widespread popular support for kneecappings. Whether it was teenagers engaging in anti-social behaviour, vandals wrecking community facilities, 'joyriders' stealing cars or burglars robbing local homes, many demanded the IRA take action.[6] As one west Belfast man put it, 'I think it is to the credit of the IRA that crime had been kept so low, because it has nothing to do with the RUC, absolutely not'.[7] Indeed, at public meetings, where anti-social behaviour was discussed, there were always those who demanded that the IRA or other groups kill, rather than wound, persistent offenders.[8] Action against so-called 'hoods' (the label given to anti-social youth in nationalist areas) could often be more popular than other aspects of the IRA's armed struggle.[9] The IRA also claimed that it was vital to combat criminality because the state was content to allow crime to flourish, to cause demoralisation in nationalist areas.[10] All the armed republican organisations, despite disputes with each other, engaged at various stages in forms of rough justice and agreed that there was a need for it.

It was also apparent from an early stage that criminal elements who engaged in disputes with republicans could face drastic consequences. In November 1970, Arthur McKenna and Alexander McVicker, well known in west Belfast for involvement in illegal gambling and small-scale extortion, were shot dead. Both men had reputations for violence and had become embroiled in a dispute with the Provisional IRA. Nevertheless, there was shock among people in Ballymurphy when they were shot.[11] At this point the Provisionals had not killed a British soldier. It was a dramatic statement that things would never be the same again in the world of crime. Similarly, while republican activists might face the prospect of a kneecapping for unauthorised robberies, for non-republicans, especially if they used the IRA's name or weapons, punishment could be far harsher. In 1978, two young Belfast men, Brian McKinney and John McClory, were abducted, shot and secretly buried by the IRA for using one of the organisation's guns in a robbery.[12] Some republicans were aware that kneecappings would not eradicate crime in nationalist areas. Noting that left-wing critics accused them of 'being mirror images of the forces they are combatting', they replied that the IRA was merely responding to community demands. During the early 1980s there were attempts to scale down punishment shootings in Belfast in favour of less drastic measures for minor offences. The IRA even admitted that its armed campaign had contributed to the 'breakdown of the social fabric of society'. This 'breakdown' had led to some alienated young people becoming involved in anti-social activities. However, by 1984, amid complaints of rising crime, the organisation claimed that the nationalist community was again demanding that 'the kid-gloves were taken off and the problem of the hoods removed'.[13]

Nowhere was the popular support for paramilitary punishment more apparent than in relation to alleged sex offenders. In December 1992, the IRA killed John Collett in Derry's Shantallow estate. He was shot in the legs with a powerful Magnum revolver; there was little doubt the intention was to cause his death.[14] Journalist Eamonn McCann described how the IRA's action had been greeted with 'savage satisfaction' by many people, as Collett was regarded as a 'sordid and malignant presence' who had raped a number of young children over the period of a year. Collett, who served a prison sentence for INLA activities, had beaten and abused his ex-wife and, in a further horrific twist, was reported to have involved a 13-year-old boy in the rape of his victims. There was little dissension from the view that the IRA had been right to shoot him, with one female trade unionist suggesting that Collett should have been tortured before being killed. Significant pressure was also put on the IRA to kill the man's teenage accomplice.[15] Despite some approval for IRA actions in these cases, revelations about the presence of abusers within its own ranks have led to republicans admitting that the organisation was 'singularly ill-equipped' to deal with this issue.[16]

So, while many supported some forms of punishment, there were worries over certain IRA actions.[17] Attitudes 'could be contradictory, with support for rough justice for offenders quickly switching to sympathy for the victims of kneecappings'. There was also the suspicion that republicans used their ability to deploy force as a form of social control. Kevin Bean has argued that the IRA had 'several related motives in dealing with crime and anti-social activity'. Policing formed 'a key part of the resistance community strategy by enabling the Provisionals to undermine the legitimacy of the state and demonstrate their role as communal defenders. However, their real concerns were not crime and social order, but control of the community and consolidating their own state forms'.[18] There were boundaries to this control, however. Hence when low-level criminal Jimmy Campbell was shot dead in Belfast in 1984, many questioned the IRA's explanation that he was a major gangland figure 'terrorizing the nationalist community'. His wife and female friends picketed polling stations with placards reading 'Beware Sinn Féin' during that year's European elections and, unusually, the IRA issued a statement retracting some of its allegations about Campbell.[19] There were similar responses to the shooting of Andrew Kearney in north Belfast in 1998. The IRA shot Kearney in the legs with a rifle, virtually guaranteeing that he would die. But Kearney, whose family were Sinn Féin supporters, was not a 'hood' and the suggestion was that his 'crime' had been to publicly humiliate a local IRA commander in a fight.[20] Kearney's death, coming in the wake of the Omagh bombing and in the midst of frantic efforts to secure peace, raised little official concern. Some critics surmised that in the context of a peace deal, shootings of working-class men like Kearney, despite being breaches of the IRA's ceasefire, would simply be ignored.[21]

Some campaigns against criminality had obvious political purposes. In October 1975, 24-year-old Sean McNamee was shot dead during a robbery by Official IRA members in Belfast. His death caused much bad feeling and the Provisional IRA decided to take advantage, launching a major attack on the Officials a month later. One man was killed and thirty wounded in a wave of shootings. The Provos justified their actions against what they called a 'criminal group' by claiming the Officials were guilty of 'murder, arson [and] gangsterism' and of bringing 'terror to the Nationalist community'.[22] But the Officials hit back and the next fortnight saw what *The Irish Times* called the 'bloodiest fighting between republicans since the Civil War' with eleven people killed and dozens injured.[23] The experience was a disaster for the

Provos. Their claims to be combating criminality were not taken seriously and the Officials retained enough popular support to ensure a backlash. The violence caused much demoralisation in nationalist areas and also contributed to the image of republicans as gangsters, feuding over territory. It fitted neatly into the British government's strategy of criminalisation.

Opposition to republican policing was also expressed by Sinn Féin's competitors within the nationalist community. During 1984, Belfast SDLP councillor Brian Feeney rejected Sinn Féin's calls for anti-crime committees by arguing that 'the Provos have no moral authority'. He claimed that the IRA sometimes encouraged the 'hoods' to riot but on other occasions told them 'they can't throw stones ... or burn cars'. Feeney opposed 'Provie peace-keeping' because the 'Provos set themselves up as the ultimate sanction ... it's the depths of hypocrisy considering they're involved in all kinds of criminal activity'.[24] He suggested that republicans were engaged in practices they denounced in others, particularly extortion and fraud.[25]

These claims were routinely rejected by republicans. But contacts and even cooperation with criminals were perhaps inevitable, particularly in the republic. In the early 1970s a substantial number of southern activists took part in operations in Northern Ireland. By the decade's end, however, the main focus of the Provisionals in the south was on maintaining arms dumps and smuggling routes, housing those on the run and, crucially, fundraising. The majority of the movement's activists were increasingly from urban working-class backgrounds. In these areas there already existed a criminal subculture with which some republicans had contact, socially or culturally, while some criminals claimed sympathy with the IRA's cause. Maintaining an armed struggle also necessitated contacts for smuggling, provision of stolen cars and ways to launder money.[26] Despite accurate fears that gardaí might use such criminal contacts to spy on republicans, a number were trusted by the IRA.[27] As one republican explained, 'you obviously don't want the person known as the local O/C [IRA commander] to be caught driving a lorry load of bleached diesel so you have to have a compromised understanding with someone else ... you don't necessarily want to be seen doing it so you have an unhealthy relationship to the underworld'.[28] This also meant, however, that there were pragmatic reasons for turning a blind eye to certain criminals or allowing them leeway in return for favours. Some might associate with the IRA in order to gain protection from criminal elements or to gain status within their communities. Having such relationships also risked dragging republicans into gangland disputes or making confrontations with criminals more likely. Indeed, the IRA and the INLA were linked to several fatal shootings of criminals in Dublin throughout the 1980s and beyond.[29]

Similar problems arose in smuggling arms. On an international scale, republicans had to engage with those criminals who also used these routes. During the border campaign the IRA began to receive weapons from a network established by Mayo native George Harrison in New York. Harrison's main contact was a gun dealer, George de Meo, who was 'on the fringe of the Mafia'.

During the 1970s some of the weapons from Harrison's network had been sourced through robberies by American gangs with links to organised crime.[30] If discovered, the potential for political embarrassment was enormous. The Irish naval service intercepted a large shipment of weapons from the United States in September 1984. The cargo had come from Boston and among those who had aided its progress was Irish-American gangster James 'Whitey' Bulger.[31] Bulger was a major figure in the Boston underworld, involved in drug dealing and numerous murders (he also provided information to the Federal Bureau of Investigation in return for immunity from prosecution).[32] Senior republican Martin Ferris, who was jailed as part of the Irish end of the gun-running operation, claimed in a TV interview in 2013 that 'if the IRA had known that at the time, would we have had anything to do with Whitey Bulger? No, absolutely not, because, as you say, he was a gangster.'[33] But it is highly unlikely that anyone active in Irish politics in Boston during the 1980s was not aware of Bulger's reputation.[34] The IRA was also linked to the robbery of $7.4 million from a security van in upstate New York in 1993. Though a former republican prisoner, Sam Millar, was involved, he asserted that the robbery had no connection to the IRA. Despite being sentenced to sixty years in prison, Millar was released and allowed to return to Ireland in 1998.[35]

All republican groups denounced drug dealing, which by the 1980s was a growing feature of Irish crime. The association with drugs was so toxic that one of the most embarrassing features of the arrest of three republicans in Colombia in 2001 was the allegation that they were in contact with the FARC, a guerrilla group allegedly linked to the cocaine trade.[36] But allegations of paramilitary involvement in the trade persist. In the case of at least one republican group, these had a basis in fact. During the 1980s the INLA tore itself apart in a series of bloody feuds. The 1987 bloodletting also produced the republican paramilitary organisation most clearly associated with criminality, the Irish People's Liberation Organisation (IPLO). The IPLO carved out an unenviable reputation in its few short years of existence. In November 1987, it killed loyalist extremist and Belfast councillor George Seawright. It also carried out openly sectarian attacks on Protestants. What marked it out, however, was its willingness to become involved with drug dealers.[37] Young criminals in Belfast were attracted to the IPLO because it offered them protection from other republicans. The IPLO in turn was happy to recruit them as foot soldiers. Republicans alleged that the group was cooperating with loyalists involved in the drugs trade. The IPLO's already grim reputation suffered a further blow during 1990 when some of its members were involved in the gang rape of a woman in Belfast. There were increasing demands for the biggest republican organisation in Belfast to do something about the IPLO.[38] It was not until late 1992, however, that the Provisional IRA moved against the group, which had itself recently split. In a major operation on 31 October over twenty IPLO members and suspected drug dealers were shot in Belfast, one fatally, while others were ordered to leave the city or be killed. The IRA asserted that the operation was aimed at 'ridding [nationalist] areas of drug pushers'.[39] Within a few days both IPLO factions disbanded, illustrating the organisation's lack of any popular base.[40]

By the early 1980s heroin use was a major problem in inner-city Dublin, with huge social consequences. In response the Concerned Parents Against Drugs (CPAD) became one of the most significant social movements to emerge from the city's working-class communities. By 1983, groups were coming together in areas blighted by heroin, holding mass meetings, marching on dealers' homes and demanding action by gardaí. Independent TD Tony Gregory and the Sinn Féin party were the only political voices who endorsed the aims of the campaigners. Many republican activists lived in the areas affected by heroin and joined the movement semi-spontaneously. As one explained, 'nobody had anybody to turn to. Nobody was turning to the guards because they were harassing you [and] they were abusing you. So communities looked after themselves. If drug dealers lived among them they were put out.'[41] Almost immediately the movement was accused by mainstream politicians of being a vigilante front for the Provisional IRA.

While Sinn Féin benefited electorally from involvement with CPAD, albeit initially in minor ways during the 1980s, the idea that it controlled the movement was incorrect. Journalist Pádraig Yeates suggested that 'the gardaí, and some politicians, are so frightened that people in these areas are organizing themselves that they claim they are being manipulated. They can't conceive that ordinary working-class people can organise themselves.'[42] The IRA initially appeared wary of direct involvement, stating in 1983 that while they had 'always been opposed to drug pushing and drug abuse and do not view lightly those who are destroying the lives of thousands of young people ... we do not believe that the solution to the problem lies in our hands. It lies with the people in the areas affected by heroin. They are the ones who can say "we don't want such people living amongst us" and who can put pressure on them to go.' While the IRA noted that the reason 'such a problem has not come about in the north is that the IRA in the course of fighting the war could not possibly tolerate it, and potential pushers were well aware of what the consequences could be for them', it stopped short of threatening similar actions in Dublin.[43] Though the organisation had carried out kneecappings in Dublin during 1982, such armed intervention had been rare, and controversial among republicans themselves.[44] Nevertheless, such was the demand for action against drugs that many people, who were not necessarily supporters of the armed struggle, still hoped that the IRA would shoot heroin dealers.

The anti-drugs movement brought the Provisional IRA into conflict with Dublin criminals.[45] A number of crime figures, led by Martin Cahill (who the media would dub 'The General'), responded to the marches and pickets of drug dealers' homes by setting up a so-called 'Concerned Criminals Action Committee'. In February 1984, two CPAD activists were shot. In response, the IRA kidnapped two of Cahill's associates, which led to the arrest of four IRA members when gardaí intercepted them. An uneasy standoff ensued, with the threat of IRA action seemingly giving CPAD a breathing space against attack by criminals. One anti-drugs activist described this as the 'big bluff'. In reality, the IRA leadership was primarily concerned with the organisation's armed struggle and was wary of becoming too deeply involved in the anti-drugs campaign. There were, indeed, many activists who were not Sinn Féin supporters who physically confronted drug dealers.[46] But the constant allegations that the IRA controlled CPAD ironically worked to make drug dealers wary of confronting it.[47]

There were several different aspects to IRA involvement in the anti-drugs movement according to André Lyder of the 1990s activist group Coalition of Communities Against Drugs (COCAD).[48] He suggested that 'the IRA has always had the reputation of being a disciplined body, and I have no doubt that it essentially is, but the occasional glimpses I had into its workings with regard to Dublin and the drugs situation revealed a Machiavellian world of subterfuge. Within this you had volunteers, at various levels in the organisation, trying to get away with as much as they possibly could without the knowledge of those higher up the chain of command.'[49] Several drug dealers, including criminals with violent reputations, were shot dead during the 1990s but the IRA only officially claimed responsibility in one instance. On 18 August 1994 they killed Martin Cahill, their last victim before the ceasefire of that year. They claimed that Cahill had connections with loyalists and had allowed the Ulster Volunteer Force to gather intelligence on republicans, which they used to attack a Dublin bar in which an IRA member was killed in May 1994.[50] But shooting Cahill also laid down a marker to Dublin's criminals, that whether on ceasefire or not, the IRA would not be a soft touch. In other cases, criminals were shot by 'IRA volunteers, non-republican anti-drug activists, or a combination of the two', though not always with authorisation from the IRA leadership. Conflicts between the IRA in Dublin and criminals continued into the twenty-first century. At a local level, there were often violent clashes, likened by one activist to 'civil war'. In Finglas, 'IRA Volunteers were physically assaulted and had their homes attacked ... of course there was a response [and] in due course it was sufficiently brutal to dissuade other than the most stupid or psychopathic from attacking anyone they thought was associated with, or under the protection of, the "Ra"'. However, in most cases these conflicts occurred away from the gaze of the media and often without sanction from the IRA's leadership.[51]

Between 1995 and 1996 a group in Northern Ireland called Direct Action Against Drugs (DAAD) claimed responsibility for killing at least six men, accusing them of being drug dealers. One of them, Francis Collins, was an ex-IRA member who had turned to crime following his release from prison. However, DAAD was simply a cover name used by the Provisional IRA in order to avoid formally breaking its ceasefire. Critics alleged it was really a way of maintaining cohesion and control during a confusing period for the movement.[52]

From 1994 onwards, the Provisional IRA's ceasefires pointed towards a slow conclusion to the conflict. Other organisations disagreed with the peace process, for a variety of reasons. Though it declared a brief ceasefire in 1995, the INLA was soon consumed by another feud. In June 1997, one of its members, John Morris, was shot dead by detectives during an attempted robbery in Dublin.[53] While the group called another ceasefire in 1998, a year later one of its volunteers, Patrick Campbell, was killed in a brutal clash with criminals in Tallaght.[54] This sparked off a round of retaliatory shootings and bombings.[55] Despite the engagement of INLA members with political initiatives in Northern Ireland, south of the border the organisation became synonymous with criminal activity.[56] During 1997–8 a significant number of Provisional IRA members left to form a new organisation. Before this group had even properly emerged as the Real IRA, one of its members, Ronan McLaughlin, had been shot and killed by gardaí during a robbery outside Dublin.[57]

As the peace process bedded down and the IRA declared a permanent end to its military operations, there was much speculation about its future role. Both republicans who opposed the peace process and long-time critics of the IRA warned that what could now emerge was 'the Rafia'. That is, an IRA which would have the capacity to combine 'political and criminal power to raise itself above its community'.[58] When the IRA was blamed for the huge Northern Bank robbery of December 2004, one former volunteer asked why carry out such an operation if 'the war is over ... Guns paid for from those [previous] bank robberies are to be melted down ... So this [Northern Bank robbery] is not about buying guns ... What is all this money needed for?'[59] Speculation suggested that the haul of an estimated £26 million would enrich individual republicans, fund a 'pension plan' for rank-and-file volunteers or become a war chest for future political battles. However, one contemporary republican source claimed that the robbery had actually 'sent a message to the British govt. that the IRA is still intact, that there are no moles in the key units, that their planning and operational skills remain high and that it would just have been as easy to blow the fuck out of London if they'd wanted to …'. Furthermore, the heist had actually 'pleased the republican troops enormously [and] put morale thru [*sic*] the roof' because there had been an 'uneasy feeling among republicans that the IRA was about to roll over and play dead to please [Ian] Paisley and for no great return'.[60] Publicly, the IRA denied any involvement.[61] But the robbery caused an intense political crisis, which, along with the murder of Belfast man Robert McCartney in early 2005, arguably speeded up the process of complete decommissioning by the IRA.[62]

Despite the formal end to the IRA's war, allegations of criminality would persist, particularly in regard to smuggling along the border.[63] Some republicans admit that 'clandestine' traditions in these areas aided the IRA's ability to operate during the conflict.[64] But others reject as black propaganda suggestions that IRA members engaged in such activities. In 2003 24-year-old IRA volunteer Keith Rogers was killed in a clash with criminals in the south Armagh village of Cullaville. The IRA claimed that Rogers died 'defending his community', with leading republican Brian Keenan describing his killers as 'vermin'.[65] Four years later another young man, 21-year-old Paul Quinn, died after a brutal beating at a farm in Monaghan. His family blamed the IRA, claiming that their son had incurred the wrath of south Armagh

republicans for defying them. Republicans in turn alleged
that Quinn's death was the result of a criminal feud. However, former Sinn Féin councillor Jim McAllister backed
the Quinn family's version of events. McAllister claimed
that some local republicans had indeed benefited from
crime. He asserted that 'the rot set in some years ago. The
IRA set up a cigarette smuggling operation in this area to
finance the struggle ... unsuspecting well-meaning people
were smuggling and taking risks to line the pockets of
these people.' McAllister suggested that 'so-called republicans' were also 'heavily involved' in importing industrial alcohol from eastern Europe which was then being
professionally bottled and sold to pubs and clubs.[66] In
February 2016 leading republican Thomas Murphy was
jailed in Dublin for tax evasion, amid more allegations
of cross-border smuggling.[67] The issue resurfaced during
the 2020 general election in the republic and is likely to
continue to do so while explanations for the persistence
of smuggling in strongly republican areas remain uncon-
vincing, or while former activists are jailed for involvement in similar activities.[68] There were also links to the
IRA alleged in the long-running dispute relating to the
Quinn family businesses along the Fermanagh–Cavan
border. One of those said to be connected to the violence,
Dublin criminal Cyril McGuinness, was suspected of having provided vehicles and other services for republicans
in the past.[69] In 2015, the garda Criminal Assets Bureau
claimed to have confiscated €28 million from over fifty
individuals with previous 'connections or associations'
to the Provisional IRA, but now involved in criminality. While the evidence pointed to the IRA having almost

completely stood down as an organisation, these individuals had made 'full use of their "legacy" reputations' in order to carve out niches in the underworld.[70] It is also significant, however, that in Northern Ireland only a very small number of prisoners released under the Good Friday Agreement later became involved in any form of illegal activity.[71]

Moreover, despite the Provisional IRA's ultimate declaration that its war was over, there were still rivals who vowed to fight on. Mainstream republicans were happy to allege criminality on the part of their 'dissident' critics.[72] In 2010 Sinn Féin's Paul Maskey accused republicans who carried out kneecappings of being mired in 'criminality, drug-dealing and extortion'. He contrasted this with the Provisional IRA for whom 'punishment attacks against criminals in the community were an option of last resort. They were carried out by a popularly based group with the consultation of the community and the aim of resolving the problem.'[73] Not all republicans agreed. In Derry, Republican Action Against Drugs (RAAD) emerged. Composed initially of ex-IRA members, motivated primarily not by hostility to the peace process but by the running down of the IRA's role in community policing, RAAD carried out dozens of shootings.[74] The Real IRA also shot dead one of its ex-members in Derry during 2010, accusing him of becoming a drug dealer, and republican organisations threatened drug dealers in Cork.[75] One anti-agreement republican suggested that 'if you took a poll and asked people do you think that the hoods and rapists should be shot they would say yes … they [the Provisionals] just walked out of our areas and left us to it'. In 2017, the *Belfast Telegraph* suggested that the police were 'losing control of North and West Belfast and dissident groups are filling that space'.[76] While not all 'dissidents' supported actions such as kneecappings, all of the armed organisations that are still active claim some form of policing role as part of their remit.[77] While communities continued to suffer from anti-social crime and despair at official responses to it, this was likely to continue.[78]

It was notable too that mainstream republicans such as Sinn Féin, when faced with accusations that demands for abolition of the Special Criminal Court meant that the party was 'soft' on lawbreaking, responded by claiming that they would actually 'crack down on crime'. Sinn Féin president Mary Lou McDonald asserted that her party 'stood shoulder to shoulder with our communities against the criminals and thugs. Sinn Féin knows we need to put a record number of gardaí onto our streets and into our communities.' McDonald suggested that 'lenient sentences are one of the reasons serious criminals feel they get away with it. They know that they will get a slap across the wrist and walk back to their lives of thuggery and crime.'[79] While demanding reform of policing, and 'intensive and systematic social investment in marginalised areas', Sinn Féin asserted that 'it is time to get tough on crime'.[80] While perhaps unusual rhetoric for a party of the left, this stance reflected the concerns of Sinn Féin's working-class base. In October 2021 the party also adjusted its long-standing policy of opposing the Special Criminal Court by accepting that on 'rare and exceptional occasions' non-jury trials were necessary.[81]

Epilogue

During 2016, Dublin was wracked by a gangland war involving the so-called Kinahan 'cartel' and members of the Hutch crime family.[1] At the time of this book's publication in 2022, nearly twenty people have died as a result. Individual republicans took part in the feud. Kevin Murray, one of the gunmen at the Regency Hotel attack which ignited the conflict, was a former IRA prisoner. The AK-47 rifles used by the Hutch faction that day were supplied by a republican group. Another Hutch associate, Michael Barr, shot dead in Dublin in 2016, was given a republican funeral in his home town of Strabane. In 2021, Jonathan Dowdall, who had briefly been a Sinn Féin councillor and was already serving a prison sentence for unrelated crimes, was charged with involvement in the Regency attack.[2] Press coverage linked various republican groups to the violence.[3] What was notable, however, was that the Kinahan organisation appeared not to fear clashes with 'dissidents', a marked difference from the heyday of the Provisional IRA. Then, no criminal gang, no matter how ruthless, would have risked an outright conflict with the Provos. By 2020, Dublin-based criminals even felt confident enough to operate in Belfast and other parts of Northern Ireland.[4] This reflected a shift in the balance of power. While the northern conflict undoubtedly influenced the rise of armed crime, drugs, particularly heroin and cocaine, had a profound and arguably greater impact on criminality in Ireland.[5] The opportunities for wealth, status and power offered by the drugs trade made involvement very attractive for a layer of youth in some communities. This, in turn, helped organised crime become a permanent fixture in the social landscape.[6] Armed republican groups, while distinct, often inhabit some of the same milieus as these criminals, and although contacts are often 'complex and complicated [and] never without a reserve of some suspicion', they almost inevitably exist.[7]

Throughout the twentieth century the majority of republican activists have not been motivated by a desire for personal advancement. Many have sacrificed far more than they have gained by involvement in republican organisations. The IRA cannot be classified simply as a criminal organisation. It has, at times, such as the during the War of Independence, been integral to the maintenance of public order. There has, indeed, often been popular support for republican policing, in its various forms. Rather, the IRA, however hostile to 'ordinary' criminals, problematises the concept of crime by calling the legitimacy of established authority into question – it exposes the fact that agreement on the nature and definition of crime is not a given and that alternative forms of authority can be established where the legitimacy of the state is weak. This can create the conditions for the boundaries between political action and crime to become porous.

A minority, in the 1920s as well as the 1990s, have taken advantage of involvement in republican politics to benefit themselves. In the twenty-first century amid further splintering, allegations of criminality multiplied. In 2002, Real IRA prisoners in Portlaoise prison complained that their 'leadership's financial motivations far outweigh their political commitment'.[8] After a split in the

Continuity IRA, Republican Sinn Féin, linked to one of the contending factions, warned of 'a new threat ... the emergence of groupings styling themselves as "Republican" but who in reality are merely using that noble title to mask their real purpose of extortion and racketeering. In some cases such groupings masquerade as anti-drugs activists, posing as "champions of the community".'[9] In 2009, the INLA 'stood down' its Dublin Brigade to investigate claims of its alleged involvement in the drugs trade.[10] In 2017, another republican group, linked to a further Continuity IRA split, asserted that 'widespread criminality has resulted in anti-national elements infiltrating the movement for their own protection', including those involved 'in the drugs trade, extortion and house-breaking'.[11] While noting that such accusations are often driven by 'innuendo, lies and propaganda', many republicans accept that 'certain individuals' connected to armed groups appear to be 'motivated solely by criminality'.[12] Explaining these developments, one republican writer argued that 'an underground army that is not meeting its military requirements suffers an inevitable descent into criminality. Criminality is the natural progression from futility.'[13] By 2022 the continual fracturing and consequent incoherence of republican military organisations suggests that links with the criminal world are likely to increase rather than decline. This, moreover, goes hand in hand with a decline in the willingness of significant political organisations to call the legitimacy of the states, north and south, into question. While armed republicans might deny criminal connections, in the absence of popular support it is likely that more and more people will accept without question the stereotypes presented in shows like *Love/Hate*.[14]

Notes

INTRODUCTION

1. *Love/Hate*, Octagon Films/RTÉ, 2010–14. The earliest version of this book began as an article written during series 3 of *Love/Hate*.

2. The label generally given to republicans who oppose the peace process and subsequent agreements.

3. 'Is *Love/Hate* Ireland's answer to *The Wire?' The Guardian*, 24 July 2013.

4. Paul Williams, *Badfellas* (Dublin: Penguin Ireland, 2011).

5. *Sunday Independent*, 26 June 2006.

6. *The Irish Times*, 5 September 2012.

7. *Sunday World*, 8 September 2013.

8. *Sunday Independent*, 9 September 2012.

9. *Irish Independent*, 5 December 2012.

10. Gene Kerrigan, *Hard Cases: True stories of Irish crime* (Dublin: Gill & Macmillan, 1996), pp. 1–90; *Irish Press*, 14 April 1988.

11. *Irish Examiner*, 11 December 2020. O'Hare was initially ostracised by other republican prisoners but was accepted back into the INLA after the Good Friday Agreement. *The Irish Times*, 9 December 2002.

12. *Irish Independent*, 13 December 2012.

13. Great Britain: Parliament: House of Commons: Northern Ireland Affairs: 'Organised Crime in Northern Ireland' (London: Westminster, 2005), p. 10.

14. Patrick Magee, *Gangsters or Guerrillas? Representations of Irish republicans in Troubles fiction* (Belfast: Beyond the Pale, 2001), p. 88.

15. Marisa McGlinchey, *Unfinished Business: The politics of 'dissident' Irish republicanism* (Manchester: Manchester University Press, 2019), pp. 174–5.

16. *An Phoblacht*, 16 November 2010.

17. Brian Campbell, Laurence McKeown and Felim O'Hagan (eds), *Nor Meekly Serve My Time: The H-Block struggle 1976–1981* (Belfast: Beyond the Pale, 1994), p. xi.

18. Ibid., pp. 1–2.

19. Kevin Bean, *The New Politics of Sinn Féin* (Liverpool: Liverpool University Press, 2007), pp. 105–6.

20. Denis O'Hearn, *Nothing But an Unfinished Song: Bobby Sands, the hunger striker who ignited a generation* (New York: Nation Books, 2006), pp. 33–4.

21. Bean, *The New Politics of Sinn Féin*, p. 108.

22. Ronnie Munck, 'Repression, Insurgency and Popular Justice: The Irish case', *Crime and Social Justice*, nos 21/2, 1984, pp. 81–94; Eric Hobsbawm, *Bandits* (London: Abacus, 2001).

23. For a variety of perspectives on IRA activity see Richard English, *Armed Struggle: A history of the IRA* (London: Macmillan, 2003); Peter Hart, *The IRA and Its Enemies: Violence and community in Cork 1916–1923* (Oxford: Oxford University Press, 1998); Tommy McKearney, *The Provisional IRA: From insurrection to parliament* (London: Pluto Press, 2011); Brendan O'Leary, 'Mission Accomplished? Looking back at the IRA', *Field Day Review*, vol. 1, 2005. pp. 217–46.

24. See the bibliography for more details.

CHAPTER 1: POLICING THE REVOLUTION

1. John Borgonovo, 'Republican Courts, Ordinary Crime, and the Irish Revolution, 1919–21', in M. de Koster, H. Leuwers, D. Luyten and X. Rousseaux (eds), *Justice in Wartime and Revolutions: Europe, 1795–1950* (Brussels: Archives Generals du Royame, 2012), pp. 49–65.

2. Pádraig Yeates, 'Who Were Dublin's Looters in 1916? Crime and society in Dublin during the Great War', *Saothar*, vol. 41, 2016, pp. 111–25.

3. Eamon Broy, Bureau of Military History witness statement (BMHWS) 1280 (Dublin: Bureau of Military History Archives Online).

4. Simon Donnelly, BMHWS 481; Richard Abbot, *Police Casualties in Ireland, 1919–1922* (Cork: Mercier Press, 2000) pp. 55–66.

5. *Irish Bulletin*, 28 November 1921.

6. Joseph O'Connor, BMHWS 601.

7. Richard Smith, BMHWS 754.

8. Patrick Cassidy, BMHWS 1017.

9. From *The Constructive Work of Dáil Éireann*, compiled and edited by Erskine Childers (Dublin: The Talbot Press, 1921), quoted in Kevin O'Sheil, BMHWS 1770.

10. *Daily Mail* articles quoted in *Irish Independent*, 20 and 24 January 1920.

11. *Freeman's Journal*, 1, 26 January 1920.

12. Ibid., 3 December 1919.

13. Seán Prendergast, BMHWS 0755.

14. *Irish Bulletin*, 28 November 1921.

15. O'Sheil, BMHWS 1770.

16. Michael Laffan, *The Resurrection of Ireland: The Sinn Féin party 1916–1923* (Cambridge: Cambridge University Press, 2005), pp. 313–18.

17. Donnelly, BMHWS 481.

18. Quoted in O'Sheil, BMHWS 1770.

19. John Dorney, 'Policing Revolutionary Dublin', *The Irish Story*, 21 June 2016.

20. There are numerous accounts in both the Bureau of Military History witness statements and the Military Service Pensions files.

21. Walter Brown, BMHWS 1436.

22. John O'Callaghan, *Limerick: The Irish revolution 1912–23* (Dublin: Four Courts Press, 2018), p. 63.

23. Charles Townshend, *The Republic: The fight for Irish independence* (London: Penguin, 2014), p. 133.

24. ICA South County Dublin Unit, Memorandum of Active and General Service (Tan War), Cowan Family Papers, University College Dublin Archives (UCDA), P34/D/45; and Christopher Crothers, Military Service Pension (MSP) 34REF210.

25. Smith, BMHWS 754.

26. Francis Carty, BMHWS 1040.

27. Cassidy, BMHWS 1017; Michael McCoy, BMHWS 1610; Joseph O'Higgins, BMHWS 507.

28. Dorney, 'Policing Revolutionary Dublin'.

29. William Desmond, BMHWS 832.

30. Townshend, *The Republic*, p. 133.

31. Royal Irish Constabulary report, 7 December 1921, in Public Record Office of Northern Ireland (PRONI), HA 5/716. I am very grateful to Patrick Mulroe for this reference.

32. Annie Deignan, MSP34REF55766; Bridget Buckley, MSP34REF30035.

33. Michael Lynch, BMHWS 50511.

34. O'Callaghan, *Limerick*, p. 64.

35. Thomas Carney, MSP34REF4491.

36. *Freeman's Journal*, 8 July 1920.

37. *Irish Bulletin*, 28 November 1921.

38. *Killarney Echo and South Kerry Chronicle*, 5 June 1920.

39. Thomas J. Martin interview, Fr Louis O'Kane Papers, Cardinal Ó Fiaich Library and Archive, Armagh.

40. James Drew, MSP34REF194.

41. Joseph Kinsella, BMHWS 0476 and MSP24SP4685.

42. Michael Fitzpatrick, BMHWS 1443.

43. James O'Toole, BMHWS 1084.

44. *Wicklow Newsletter*, 6 November 1920.

45. Donnelly, BMHWS 481.

46. Henry S. Murray, BMHWS 601.

47. O'Connor, BMHWS 601.

48. Carty, BMHWS 1040.

49. *Strabane Chronicle*, 14 August 1920 and *Nationalist and Leinster Times*, 4 September 1920.

50. Prendergast, BMHWS 0755.

51. Denis McDonnell, BMHWS 1273.

52. Laurence Dineen, MSPREF34015; Christopher Lynch, MSP34REF496; Martin Kelly, MSP34REF32183.

53. *The Irish Times*, 22 November 1919.

54. Arthur Mitchell, *Revolutionary Government in Ireland: Dáil Éireann 1919–1922* (Dublin: Gill & Macmillan, 1995), pp. 150–4.

55. Áine Ceannt, BMHWS 264.

56. Jeremiah Galvin, MSP34REF26252.

57. Lynch, BMHWS 50511.

58. Edward O'Sullivan, BMHWS 1501.

59. Charles Zemmitt, MSP34REF1773.

60. *Old Ireland*, 7 August 1920. They retained £28 for 'expenses incurred in tracing the thieves'. Thanks to Peter Rigney for this information.

61. Seán Boylan, BMHWS 1715.

62. Thomas Treacy, BMHWS 1093.

63. Joseph Stanford, BMHWS 1334.

64. Marie Coleman, *County Longford and the Irish Revolution, 1910–1923* (Dublin: Irish Academic Press, 2003), p. 143.

65. Arthur Vincent to Richard Mulcahy, 30 August 1921, in Mulcahy Papers, P7/A/23.

66. Mitchell, *Revolutionary Government in Ireland*, p. 152.

67. Liam O'Carroll, BMHWS 594; *Evening Herald*, 14 October 1920.

68. Sam McGrath, 'The Sons of Dawn – Dublin's "Midnight Crawlers"', *Come Here to Me*, 12 September 2017; O'Carroll, BMHWS 594; Michael Douglas, MSP34REF950.

69. Townshend, *The Republic*, pp. 130–4.

70. Desmond, BMHWS 832.

71. Peter Hart, *The IRA and Its Enemies: Violence and community in Cork 1916–1923* (Oxford: Oxford University Press, 1998), pp. 148–52.

72. Brian Hanley, '"The Layers of an Onion": Reflections on 1913, class and the memory of the Irish revolution', in Conor McNamara and Pádraig Yeates (eds), *The Dublin Lockout 1913: New perspectives on class war & its legacy* (Dublin: Irish Academic Press, 2017), pp. 144–60.

73. Con Meany, BMHWS 787.

74. O'Callaghan, *Limerick*, p. 93.

75. *Limerick Leader*, 2 July 1920. See also *Irish Bulletin*, 7 August 1920.

76. *Tuam Herald*, 19 June 1920.

77. Sinéad Joy, *The IRA in Kerry 1916–1921* (Cork: The Collins Press, 2005), p. 44; *The Kerryman*, 19 June 1920.

78. Thomas Lavin, BMHWS 1001. Aoife Breathnach makes the point that terms such as 'tramp' and 'tinker' were often used interchangeably but referred to distinct groups of people; Aoife Breathnach, *Becoming Conspicuous: Irish Travellers, society and the state, 1922–70* (Dublin: UCD Press, 2006), pp. 38–9.

79. Joseph G. O'Sullivan, MSP34REF627.

80. O/C Second Southern Division to D/Information, 12 July 1921, Richard Mulcahy Papers, UCDA, P7/A/22. Seamus Babington recounts how this suspicion of 'tramps' could lead to innocent men being accused of spying; BMHWS 1595.

81. Brown, BMHWS 1436.

82. Terry Dunne, 'The Agrarian Movement of 1920: Cattle drivers, marauders, terrorists and hooligans', *History Ireland*, vol. 28, 2020, pp. 30–3.

83. Emmet O'Connor, *A Labour History of Ireland 1824–2000* (Dublin: UCD Press, 2011), p. 115.

84. Borgonovo, 'Republican Courts'.

85. Meany, BMHWS 787; Donal Ó Drisceoil, 'Storm Centre: The Brigade Activity Reports from Cork', in *The Military Service (1916–1923) Pensions Collection: The Brigade Activity Reports* (Dublin: The Military Archives, 2018), pp. 108–15.

86. Christopher O'Keeffe, BMHWS 761.

87. *Irish Bulletin*, 14, 16 June 1920.

88. Luke Duffy, BMHWS 661.

89. *Leinster Express*, 12 February 1921. I am grateful to Terry Dunne for this reference.

90. Seán Farrelly, BMHWS 1734. See also Myles Dungan, *Four*

Killings: Land hunger, murder and a family in the Irish revolution (London: Head of Zeus, 2021).

91. Seamus Finn, BMHWS 1060 and Patrick Loughran, BMHWS 1624; David M. Doyle and Liam O'Callaghan, *Capital Punishment in Independent Ireland: A social, legal and political history* (Liverpool: Liverpool University Press, 2019), pp. 21–2.

92. Michael Finnegan, 'Four Killings', unpublished manuscript, Dublin, 2021. I am grateful to Scott Millar for access to this account.

93. Michael Davern, BMHWS 1348.

94. *Irish Bulletin*, 28 November 1921.

95. Frank Henderson, BMHWS 821.

96. Seamus Fitzgerald, BMHWS 1737.

97. T.K. Wilson, *Frontiers of Violence: Conflict and identity in Ulster and Upper Silesia 1918–1922* (Oxford: Oxford Historical Monographs, 2010), pp. 6, 120–1.

98. Marie Coleman, 'Violence Against Women in the Irish War of Independence, 1919–1921', in Diarmaid Ferriter and Susannah Riordan (eds), *Years of Turbulence: The Irish revolution and its aftermath* (Dublin: UCD Press, 2015), pp. 137–56.

99. Ann Matthews, *Renegades: Irish republican women 1900–1922* (Cork: Mercier Press, 2010), pp. 266–82; Linda Connolly, 'Sexual Violence in the Irish Civil War: A forgotten war crime?', *Women's History Review*, vol. 30, 2021, pp. 126–43. See also Linda Connolly, 'Towards a Further Understanding of the Sexual and Gender-based Violence Women Experienced in the Irish Revolution', in Linda Connolly (ed.), *Women and the Irish Revolution* (Newbridge: Irish Academic Press, 2020), pp. 103–28. For an analysis of contemporary narratives surrounding gender and sexual violence, see Susan Byrne, '"Keeping Company With the Enemy": Gender and sexual violence against women during the Irish War of Independence and Civil War, 1919–1923', *Women's History Review*, vol. 30, 2021, pp. 108–25.

100. Eunan O'Halpin, 'Counting Terror: Bloody Sunday and the dead of the Irish revolution', in David Fitzpatrick (ed.), *Terror in Ireland, 1916–1923* (Dublin: The Lilliput Press, 2012), pp. 141–57.

101. Townshend, *The Republic*, pp. 71–2, 90–2; Patrick O'Sullivan

Greene, *Crowdfunding the Revolution: The First Dáil Loan and the battle for Irish independence* (Dublin: Eastwood, 2020).

102. Directorate of Intelligence, 'Report on Revolutionary Organisations in the United Kingdom', 12 May 1921, CAB 24_123_43, The National Archives (UK).

103. *An t-Óglách*, 6 May 1922.

104. Brian Hughes, *Defying the IRA? Intimidation, coercion, and communities during the Irish revolution* (Liverpool: Liverpool University Press, 2016), pp. 91–100.

105. Lynch, BMHWS 50511.

106. Cassidy, BMHWS 1017.

107. Pádraig Yeates, *A City in Turmoil: Dublin 1919–21* (Dublin: Gill & Macmillan, 2015), p. 225.

108. Laurence Corbally, MSP34REF1390; *Irish Independent*, 25 March 1922.

109. Seamus Connelly, BMHWS 976.

110. Michael V. O'Donoghue, BMHWS 1741.

111. Edmund Tobin, BMHWS 1451.

112. Patrick Kerin, BMHWS 977.

113. Edward O'Sullivan, MSP34REF1824.

114. Patrick Wilcox, BMHWS 1529.

115. Michael Desmond, BMHWS 1338.

116. Cormac O'Malley and Vincent Keane (eds), *The Men Will Talk to Me: Mayo interviews by Ernie O'Malley* (Cork: Mercier Press, 2014), p. 315.

117. James Redican, MSP34REF521; Ciarán Murray, 'The Bolsheviki Bookies', *Come Here to Me*, 29 March 2017.

118. Yeates, *A City in Turmoil*, pp. 226–9.

119. *Belfast News Letter*, 8 January, 5 March 1921.

120. D.M. Leeson, *The Black and Tans: British police and Auxiliaries in the Irish War of Independence, 1920–1921* (Oxford: Oxford University Press, 2011), pp. 83–4, 121–4.

121. *Anglo-Celt*, 29 January 1921.

122. *Freeman's Journal*, 4 June 1921.

123. *The Irish Times*, 23 September 1921.

124. Dan Breen, BMHWS 1739.

125. Maria Luddy, *Prostitution and Irish Society, 1800–1940* (Cambridge: Cambridge University Press, 2007), pp. 156–93. Indeed one account suggests the IRA in Cork city rounded up women engaged in prostitution and brought them to a Magdalene laundry. Mark Bulik, *Ambush on 84th St: When the Irish revolution came to New York* (New York: Fordham University Press, forthcoming).

126. Treacy, BMHWS 1093; S. Lanigan to M. Collins, 21 June 1919, in Richard Mulcahy Papers, UCDA, P7/A1.

127. James Delaney, BMHWS 1360. 'Darby' may in fact have been 'Darkie the Coon' (Isaac Bogard), a Jewish gang leader in the East End; James Morton, *East End Gangland* (London: Sphere, 2000), pp. 126–9.

128. Denis Carr, MSP34REF2743. I am very grateful to Sam McGrath for this reference. For a discussion of these gangs see Heather Shore, *London's Criminal Underworlds c. 1720 – c. 1930* (London: Palgrave, 2015).

129. Denis Kelleher, Ernie O'Malley Notebooks, UCDA, P17b/107.

130. Richard Walsh, BMHWS 400.

131. Denis Sugrue, MSP34REF64446.

132. James W. Cunningham, BMHWS 922.

133. Gilbert Barrington, BMHWS 773.

134. Joseph Good, BMHWS 338.

135. Report on Hamburg (N/D), Maurice Twomey Papers, UCDA, P69/217.

136. Dr Paddy Daly, O'Malley Notebooks, UCDA, P17b/136.

137. 'Deverantis Story' as told to Dr Moloney in Éamon de Valera Papers, UCDA, P150/668.

138. Walsh, BMHWS 400.

139. See for example pension applications from William Hogan, MSP3425163; Peter Fox, MSP34REF134; William Dwane, MSP34REF34016; and Christopher Moriarty, MSP24SP2560.

140. *Sligo Champion*, 7 January 1922.

141. Laffan, *The Resurrection of Ireland*, p. 280

142. *An t-Óglach*, 1 September 1920.

143. General Orders, Republican Police, Collins Papers, Military Archives, IE_MA_CP_05_O1_27.

CHAPTER 2: CONTROL, CHAOS AND CRIMINALITY: THE CIVIL WAR AND AFTER

1. *Evening Herald*, 16 January 1922.

2. Michael Hopkinson, *Green Against Green: The Irish Civil War* (Dublin: Gill & Macmillan, 1989), p. 91.

3. Brian McCarthy, *The Civic Guard Mutiny* (Cork: Mercier Press, 2012).

4. *The Irish Times*, 30 September 1921.

5. John Gleeson, MSP34REF791.

6. *Irish Bulletin*, 16 November 1921.

7. Patrick Kelly, BMHWS 781.

8. *Irish Bulletin*, 16 November 1921.

9. *Sligo Champion*, 7 January 1922.

10. John McCoy, BMHWS 492.

11. Sam McGrath, 'Claude Gunner's Gang', *Come Here to Me*, 23 July 2018; Kelly, BMHWS 781; Michael Oman, MSP34REF10143. An outfit known as the 'Anderson Gang' were held at 144 Great Brunswick Street. Ernest F. Piggot, MSP34REF4137.

12. Michael Foy, *The Aftermath of Revolution: Sligo 1921–23* (Dublin: UCD Press, 2000), p. 158.

13. Hughes, *Defying the IRA?*, pp. 173–4.

14. Michael Davern, BMHWS 1348.

15. *Workers' Republic*, 19, 26 November 1921.

16. Foy, *The Aftermath of Revolution*, p. 163

17. *An t-Óglách*, 3 February 1922.

18. *Freeman's Journal*, 7, 17 January 1922.

19. Ibid., 22 February 1922.

20. Borgonovo, 'Republican Courts', p. 63.

21. *Irish Independent*, 14 March 1922.

22. Foy, *The Aftermath of Revolution*, p. 164; Hopkinson, *Green Against Green*, pp. 89–90.

23. John Dorney, *The Civil War in Dublin: The fight for the Irish capital 1922–24* (Newbridge: Merrion Press, 2017), p. 46.

24. *Irish Independent*, 22 July 1922.

25. Dorney, *The Civil War in Dublin*, p. 56.

26. *Belfast News Letter*, 15 April 1922.

27. Ibid., 13 June 1922; Kieran Glennon, 'Belfast Republicans and the Treaty Split of 1922', *The Irish Story* (website), 26 March 2022.

28. Townshend, *The Republic*, pp. 423–7.

29. Joy, *The IRA in Kerry*, pp. 112–13.

30. Seán Moylan, BMHWS 0838.

31. Gavin M. Foster, *The Irish Civil War and Society: Politics, class and conflict* (Basingstoke: Palgrave Macmillan, 2015), pp. 38–9.

32. John M. Regan, *The Irish Counter-Revolution 1921–1936* (Dublin: Gill & Macmillan, 1999), pp. 103–4.

33. Foster, *The Irish Civil War and Society*, pp. 60–1.

34. *Irish Independent*, 17 February 1922.

35. Gerald Feeney, MSP34REF41725; John Peyton, MSP34REF1151; Thomas Carney, MSP34REF4491.

36. Pat McCarthy, *The Irish Revolution: Waterford 1912–23* (Dublin: Four Courts Press, 2015), p. 92; Michael Bishop, MSP24SP11719; Sean Hyde, MSP34REF16364.

37. John J. Cox, MSP2D496.

38. Patrick Dunleavy, MSPWSP1721.

39. *Freeman's Journal*, 15 March 1924.

40. John Bergin, MSP2D12.

41. John Borgonovo, *The Battle for Cork: July–August 1922* (Cork: Mercier Press, 2011), p. 36.

42. Ibid.; McCarthy, *The Irish Revolution*, pp. 99–100.

43. *An t-Óglách*, 6 May 1922. There were also incidents of pro-treaty IRA men engaging in sectarian intimidation; Garda report, D/Justice 2008/117/565–7, NAI, 31 July 1935.

44. Conor McNamara, *War and Revolution in the West of Ireland: Galway, 1913–1922* (Newbridge: Irish Academic Press, 2018), pp. 179–81.

45. Dorney, *The Civil War in Dublin*, p. 55; Robert Lynch, 'Explaining the Altnaveigh Massacre', *Éire-Ireland*, fall/winter 2010, pp. 184–210.

46. Connolly, 'Sexual Violence in the Irish Civil War', p. 2. In this case the work of Claudia Card is relevant; Claudia Card, 'Rape as a Weapon of War', *Hypatia*, vol. 11, no. 4, 1996, pp. 5–18.

47. Matthews, *Renegades*, pp. 266–82; Lindsey Earner-Byrne, 'The Rape of Mary M: A microhistory of sexual violence and moral redemption in 1920s Ireland', *Journal of the History of Sexuality*, vol. 24, 2015, pp. 75–98; Gemma Clark, 'Violence Against Women in the Irish Civil War, 1922–3: Gender-based harm in global perspective', *Irish Historical Studies*, vol. 44, 2020, pp. 75–90.

48. Carty, BMHWS 1040.

49. Richard Walsh, BMHWS 400.

50. *An t-Óglách*, 6 May 1922.

51. Adrian Grant, *Derry: The Irish revolution, 1912–23* (Dublin: Four Courts Press, 2018), p. 135.

52. Gerard Noonan, *The IRA in Britain, 1919–1923: 'In the heart of enemy lines'* (Liverpool: Liverpool University Press, 2014), p. 260.

53. Bartley Igoe, MSP34REF54160.

54. Uinseann MacEoin, *The IRA in the Twilight Years, 1923–1948* (Dublin: Argenta 1997), p. 179.

55. *The Irish Times*, 30 July 1924.

56. Terence Dooley, *Monaghan: The Irish revolution, 1912–23* (Dublin: Four Courts Press, 2017), p. 107.

57. Brigade Adjutant to O/Cs, FitzGerald Papers, P80/770 (12), 8 September 1922.

58. *Iris an Arm*, FitzGerald Papers, UCDA, P80/728, 2 October 1922.

59. Officer Commanding (O/C) to South Wexford Units, FitzGerald Papers, UCDA, P80/770 (7), 6 September 1922.

60. Chief of Staff (C/S) to O/Cs All Divisions, Maurice Twomey Papers, UCDA, P69/2 (25), 24 August 1922.

61. Tom Derrig, Adjutant General (A/G) IRA to O/Cs, FitzGerald Papers, UCDA, P80/781, 27 December 1922.

62. Michael Cull, MSPDP2370; Frank Dolphin, MSP24SP3920.

63. *Anglo-Celt*, 10 February 1923; John Dorney, 'The Tragedies of Ballyconnell', *The Irish Story*, 19 June 2014. The attacks are remembered by Fermanagh unionists as sectarian in nature, but both Catholics and Protestants in Ballyconnell were targeted; Edward Burke, *An Army of Tribes: British army cohesion, deviancy and murder in Northern Ireland* (Liverpool: Liverpool University Press, 2018), pp. 240–1.

64. Luke Burke (who used the name Henry Keenan), MSPDP903 and Michael Grealy, MSPDP1835; Breen Murphy, 'The Government's Executions Policy during the Irish Civil War 1922–23', unpublished PhD thesis, NUI Maynooth, 2010, p. 267.

65. Michael Keane, 'Dependency claims for the Civil War Executed in the Military Service (1916–1923) Pensions Collection', *History Ireland*, vol. 26, March/April 2018, pp. 42–5.

66. Murphy, *The Government's Executions Policy*, p. 199.

67. *The Irish Times*, 7 December 1922. I am grateful to Pádraig Ó Ruairc for this reference.

68. Foy, *The Aftermath of Revolution*, p. 170.

69. Ibid., p. 171; *Sligo Champion*, 28 October 1922.

70. *Connacht Tribune*, 9 September 1922.

71. *Freeman's Journal*, 18 January 1923.

72. *Irish Independent*, 2 May 1923.

73. *Connacht Tribune*, 27 January 1923.

74. Kieran Glennon, *From Pogrom to Civil War: Tom Glennon and the Belfast IRA* (Cork: Mercier Press, 2013), pp. 228–9.

75. *Éire*, 3 March 1923.

76. Anne Dolan and C.H. O'Malley (eds), *'No Surrender Here!' The*

Civil War papers of Ernie O'Malley 1922–24 (Dublin: The Lilliput Press, 2007), p. 299.

77. Dorney, *The Civil War in Dublin*, p. 262.

78. Ibid., p. 252; 'Summary of Operations for Fortnight Ending 21st April 1923', Twomey Papers, UCDA, P69/20 (449).

79. *Freeman's Journal*, 3 October 1922; Dorney, *The Civil War in Dublin*, p. 183.

80. 'Murders and Principal Outrages Committed by Irregulars since the "Cease Fire" Order, April, 1925', Department of the Taoiseach (D/T) S5864A, National Archives of Ireland (NAI) September 1931; Dorney, *The Civil War in Dublin*, p. 260.

81. Dorney, *The Civil War in Dublin*, p. 262.

82. *Connacht Tribune*, 2 June 1923.

83. *Freeman's Journal*, 31 May 1923.

84. *The Irish Times*, 29 March and 9 May 1924.

85. *Freeman's Journal*, 24 July 1923.

86. *Military Service Pensions Blog*, 'Killing Their Own – Philip Doyle and Jeremiah Gaffney', 14 November 2019.

87. Dorney, *The Civil War in Dublin*, p. 260.

88. Report by Eoin O'Duffy for Cabinet, FitzGerald Papers, UCDA, P80/851 (5), 8 April 1929.

89. Christopher Crothers, MSP34REF210; Joe Mooney, 'A Family at War with the Empire: Christy and "Dina" Crothers of the Irish Citizen Army', *East Wall for All*, 4 April 2016.

90. *Freeman's Journal*, 27 October 1923.

91. Ibid., 21 November 1923.

92. Ibid., 30 November 1923.

93. *The Irish Times*, 12 July 1924.

94. *Irish Independent*, 2 August 1924.

95. Dorney, *The Civil War in Dublin*, p. 261.

96. Michael Watchorn, MSP2410440.

97. James Freyne, MSPW1924A1.

98. John Reynolds, MSP24SP4473.

99. James Casey, MSP4D34.

100. Cases included in Hugh Martin, MSP24B717.

101. *Éire*, 24 November and 15 December 1923.

102. Barry McLoughlin, *Left to the Wolves: Irish victims of Stalinist terror* (Dublin: Irish Academic Press, 2007), pp. 219–83.

103. Jim Phelan, *The Name's Phelan: The first autobiography of Jim Phelan* (Newtownards: Blackstaff Press, 1993).

104. *The Irish Times*, 10 July 1923.

105. Hugh Martin, MSP24SP11738. See also Breandán Mac Suibhne, 'The Generation that Lost: The Ulster Bank, Ardara, County Donegal, 16 June 1921, and long after, and far away', in Patrick Mannion and Fearghal McGarry (eds), *A Global History of Irish Revolution* (New York: New York University Press, 2022).

106. *The Irish Times*, 19 November 1924.

107. Ibid., 12 May and 17 July 1924.

108. Though reflecting the confusing times, Keogh's brother Jim had been shot dead in May 1922 while part of an IRA unit attempting to evict squatters; James Keogh MSPDP7620.

109. See reports in *The Irish Times* of a man shot dead during a robbery in Dublin, 2 January 1926; an Omagh bank raid, 11 January 1926; a Carlow armed robbery, 1 October 1926; an Athenry armed robbery, 22 November 1926; and a Cork hold-up, 4 December 1926. For the Doyle murder, see 'Murders and Principal Outrages' (NAI).

110. *Leitrim Observer*, 28 January 1927.

111. *The Irish Times*, 29 January and 7 February 1927.

112. *The Nation*, 6 August 1927.

113. Brian Hanley, *The IRA: 1926–1936* (Dublin: Four Courts Press, 2002), pp. 44–5.

114. Tom Mahon and James J. Gillogly, *Decoding the IRA* (Cork: Mercier Press, 2008) pp. 245–80.

115. Hanley, *The IRA*, pp. 167–8; Report on IRA Convention, August 1934, Jus8/2008/117/740 NAI.

116. Minutes of 1933 General Army Convention, Twomey Papers, UCDA, P69/187 (100), p. 15.

117. Inquiry in Capture of St Enda's Dump, Twomey Papers, UCDA, P69/57 (2–9), 1926.

118. *The Irish Times*, 25 January 1930; A/G to O/C Dublin, Twomey Papers, UCDA, P69/151 (231–2), 12 February 1930.

119. Hanley, *The IRA*, p. 49.

120. Garda Superintendent's Report, FitzGerald Papers, UCDA, P80/851 (15), 16 May 1929.

121. *Tipperary Star*, 15 June 1929.

122. Garda Superintendent's Report, FitzGerald Papers, UCDA, P80/851 (7), 23 April 1929.

123. Michael Moroney, *George Plant and the Rule of Law: The Devereux affair 1940–42* (Tipperary: County Tipperary Historical Society, 1989).

CHAPTER 3: RETHINKING AND RE-ORGANISATION: FROM THE 1930S TO THE NORTHERN WAR

1. Bill Kissane, 'Defending Democracy? The legislative response to political extremism in the Irish Free State, 1922–39', *Irish Historical Studies*, vol. 34, 2004, pp. 156–74.

2. Hanley, *The IRA*, pp. 123–43.

3. There has been little scholarly work on these so-called 'Broy Harriers'. However, the Military Service Pensions files are making it possible to trace the careers of the ex-IRA men who became detectives. See Denis O'Brien, MSP34REF1281.

4. *Irish Press*, 30 March 1935.

5. Kissane, 'Defending Democracy?', pp. 167–72.

6. Donal Fallon, 'Newsboys and the "Animal Gang" in 1930s Dublin', in David Convery (ed), *Locked Out: A century of Irish working-class life* (Dublin: Irish Academic Press, 2013), pp. 93–108.

7. Garda report, 12 September 1934, Jus8/67, NAI.

8. *An Phoblacht*, 29 September 1934.

9. Fergus Whelan, 'Street War', *Look Left*, vol. 2, no. 10, 2012, pp. 8–10.

10. *The Irish Times*, 15 February 1938.

11. Newsboys had attacked the Republican Congress office during the 1934 strike as well. Hanley, *The IRA*, pp. 83–4.

12. Brian Hanley, *The IRA: A documentary history 1916–2005* (Dublin: Gill & Macmillan, 2010), pp. 97–118.

13. For Germany, see David O'Donoghue, *The Devil's Deal: The IRA, Nazi Germany and the double life of Jim O'Donovan* (Dublin: New Island, 2010).

14. *The Irish Times*, 24 June 1936 and 8 November 1945.

15. Department of Justice, 'Confidential Departmental Notes on Events, Jan. 1931 – Dec. 1940', UCDA, P67/534, p. 86I.

16. Ibid., p. 86.

17. Department of Justice, 'Notes on IRA Activities, 1941–1947', MacEntee Papers, UCDA, P67/550, pp. 11–12.

18. Robert J. Murphy, MSP24SP9177.

19. *The Irish Times*, 6 September 1941.

20. 'Notes on IRA Activities', pp. 15–17.

21. *The Irish Times*, 23 January 1942.

22. 'Notes on IRA Activities', pp. 57–63.

23. *Irish Independent*, 25 June 1943; Barry McLaughlin and Emmet O'Connor, *In Spanish Trenches: The minds and deeds of the Irish who fought for the Spanish republic in the Spanish Civil War* (Dublin: UCD Press, 2020) p. 367.

24. J. Bowyer Bell, *The Secret Army: The IRA from 1916* (Dublin: The Academy Press, 1979), p. 217.

25. *United Irishman*, May 1950.

26. Department of Justice, Memorandum for Government, D/T 98/6/494, NAI, 20 November 1961.

27. Department of Justice, Review of Unlawful and Allied Organisations, D/T 98/6/495, NAI, 1 December 1964 to 21 November 1966.

28. Chris Connolly has written in more detail about this. See *The Irish Times*, 4 January 2014.

29. J. Bowyer Bell, *IRA Tactics and Targets* (Dublin: Poolbeg Press, 1990), p. 93.

30. *Belfast Telegraph*, 17 February 1966.

31. Department of Justice, Review of Unlawful and Allied Organisations D/T 98/6/495, NAI.

32. Minutes of meeting, 29–30 August 1967. Private source. Copy deposited at UCDA.

33. Ibid.

34. Memorandum for government in relation to IRA, Department Justice (D/J), 2000/36/3 (NAI), 18 March 1969.

35. Brian Hanley, '"The Needs of the People": The IRA considers its future, 1967–68', *Saothar*, vol. 38, 2013, pp. 83–90.

36. *Irish Independent*, 6 May 1967.

37. *Daily Telegraph*, 10 January 1967.

38. *The Irish Times*, 28 February 1967.

39. Brian Hanley and Scott Millar, *The Lost Revolution: The story of the Official IRA and the Workers' Party* (Dublin: Penguin Ireland, 2009), pp. 63, 117.

40. *Irish News*, 7 March 1969.

41. Hanley and Millar, *The Lost Revolution*, p. 143. For a sympathetic view of the group see Healy, *Saor Éire*.

42. *The Irish Times*, 2 January 1970.

43. Derek Dunne and Gene Kerrigan, *Round Up the Usual Suspects: The Cosgrave coalition and Nicky Kelly* (Dublin: Gill & Macmillan, 1984), p. 72.

44. Sean Flynn and Pádraig Yeates, *Smack! The criminal drugs racket in Ireland* (Dublin: Gill & Macmillan, 1985), p. 25.

45. Vicky Conway, *Policing Independent Ireland: A history of An Garda Síochána* (London: Routledge, 2013), p. 113.

46. Kieran Conway, *Southside Provisional: From freedom fighter to the Four Courts* (Dublin: Orpen Press, 2014), p. 20.

47. *Irish Press*, 4 April 1970. Both the Officials and newly formed Provisionals denied any involvement in the shooting.

48. *Hibernia*, 17 April 1970.

49. *The Irish Times*, 14 and 16 October 1970.

50. *Irish Press*, 15 and 17 May 1969.

51. *The Irish Times*, 21 May 1969.

52. Memorandum for government in relation to IRA, Department Justice (D/J), 2000/36/3 (NAI), 18 March 1969.

53. *The Irish Times*, 6 July 1972.

54. Ibid., 27 October 1973.

55. Ibid., 1 October 1971.

56. Former Provisional IRA activist Kieran Conway asserts that in potentially embarrassing cases the movement 'lied whenever we thought we could get away with it'. Conway, *Southside Provisional*, p. 93.

57. Minutes of Official IRA General Army Convention, October 1972, in Hanley, *The IRA: A documentary history*, pp. 177–9.

58. Official Republican Movement, 'The State of the Movement in South Down and Armagh', August 1972 (private source – copy deposited at UCD Archives).

59. Hanley and Millar, *The Lost Revolution*, pp. 230–1.

60. Northern Ireland Office report, Public Record Office of Northern Ireland, PCC/1/5/28, 26 October 1976.

61. OIRA leadership discussion document, 1977 (private source – copy deposited at UCD Archives).

62. *The Irish Times*, 9 March 1982.

63. *Irish News*, 27 April and 15 December 1977.

64. *The Irish Times*, 5 September 1978.

65. Gerard O'Brien, *An Garda Síochána and the Scott Medal* (Dublin: Four Courts Press, 2008), pp. 103–4.

66. *The Irish Times*, 10 October 1978.

67. *United Irishman*, March 1976.

68. Hanley and Millar, *The Lost Revolution*, pp. 519–45.

69. Joe Brennan, *Superdollar: A North Korean conspiracy* (Belfast: OJM, 2011).

70. Quoted in *'The Man with the Hat': The revolutionary life and times of Sean Garland*, Gansee Films, dir. Kevin Brannigan, 2018.

71. See, for example, 'The Secret World of SFWP', *Magill*, April 1982; *The Irish Times*, 26 October 1992.

72. Hanley and Millar, *The Lost Revolution*, pp. 546–87.

73. Brian Hanley, *The Impact of the Troubles on the Republic of Ireland, 1968–79* (Manchester: Manchester University Press, 2018), pp. 70–1.

74. *This Week*, 12 November 1971.

75. *Sunday Press*, 20 May 1973.

76. *The Irish Times*, 13 and 21 October 1972.

77. *Time Out*, 4 April 1974.

78. It would seem that the Provisionals did not officially authorise armed robberies in the republic until 1973. See Paul McGuill, 'Political Violence in the Republic of Ireland 1969–1997', unpublished MA thesis, University College Dublin, 1998, p. 84.

79. *Fortnight*, 12 November 1971.

80. *Irish Independent*, 15 October 1971.

81. Conway, *Southside Provisional*, pp. 39–44.

82. Patrick Radden Keefe, *Say Nothing: A true story of murder and memory in Northern Ireland* (London: William Collins, 2019), p. 53.

83. For a description of one such robbery in 1973 see Brendan Hughes and Douglas Dalby, *Up Like a Bird: The rise and fall of an IRA commander* (Castleisland: Time Warp Books, 2021), pp. 34–40.

84. J.J. Barrett, *Martin Ferris: Man of Kerry* (Dingle: Brandon, 2005), pp. 52–7. For the Shannon robbery see also Hughes and Dalby, *Up Like a Bird*, pp. 277–80.

85. *Cork Examiner*, 11 July 1977; Gearóid Ó Faoleán, *A Broad Church: The Provisional IRA in the Republic of Ireland 1969–1980* (Newbridge: Merrion Press, 2019), pp. 118–19.

86. *New Statesman*, 1 December 1972.

87. Derek Dunne, 'A Very Special Criminal Court', *Magill*, 15 May 1985.

88. 'Conditions in Portlaoise Prison', D/T 2007/116/396, NAI. Thanks to Ciara Molloy for this reference.

89. 'Level of Violence in 26 Counties Resulting in Declaration of State of Emergency', D/T 2006/133/581, NAI, September 1976.

90. Military Intelligence report, D/J 2008/79/3109, NAI, 15 February 1977.

91. Some were also carried out by dissident members of republican groups. See Hughes and Dalby, *Up Like a Bird*, pp. 47–8.

92. *The Irish Times*, 29 November 1977.

93. *Evening Press*, 3 October 1978. The culprits were believed to be County Derry IRA men operating in Donegal. Patrick Mulroe, *Bombs, Bullets and the Border: Policing Ireland's frontier. Irish security policy, 1969–1978* (Newbridge: Irish Academic Press, 2017), pp. 212–13.

94. *Magill*, December 1978.

95. Mulroe, *Bombs, Bullets and the Border*, p. 181.

96. *Magill*, December 1978.

97. Ibid., September 1979.

98. *The Irish Times*, 3 March and 9 April 1975.

99. IRSP, *Framed Through the Special Criminal Court: The 'great train robbery' trial* (Dublin: Starry Plough Publications, 1979).

100. Dunne and Kerrigan, *Round Up the Usual Suspects*, pp. 261–5.

101. Jack Holland and Henry McDonald, *INLA: Deadly divisions* (Dublin: Torc, 1994), pp. 128–9.

102. *Magill*, August 1978.

103. Thomas McNulty, *Exiled: 40 years an exile* (Monaghan: TMN Publications, 2013), p. 102.

104. Richard O'Rawe, *Blanketmen: An untold story of the H-Block hunger strike* (Dublin: New Island, 2005), pp. 3–4.

105. *Donegal News*, 27 February 1979.

106. Magee, *Gangsters or Guerrillas?*, pp. 83–4.

107. Brigadier General James Glover, 'Northern Ireland: Future terrorist trends', in Sean Cronin, *Irish Nationalism: Its roots and ideology* (Dublin: The Academy Press, 1980), pp. 339–57.

108. Ó Faoleán, *A Broad Church*, p. 78.

109. Indeed, robberies in the north were much more likely to involve deadly violence; see for example the killing of RUC officer William Elliot by the OIRA during September 1974 or of John Brown, shot dead during an INLA post office robbery in December 1980. Similarly, a number of those taking part in robberies were also shot dead; three men were killed by an undercover British army unit in Belfast during January 1990, for example. The Sutton Index of deaths in the conflict lists over forty people who died during robberies in Northern Ireland: https://cain.ulster.ac.uk/sutton/search.html.

110. *The Irish Times*, 4 August 1973.

111. Ibid., 3 September 1974.

112. *Irish Press*, 12 September 1975. The robbers were ex-members of the Official IRA.

113. *The Irish Times*, 18 December 1976.

114. *Donegal News*, 4 February 1978.

115. *Munster Express*, 10 August 1979.

116. *Irish Press*, 9 July and 15 October 1980.

117. Ibid., 9 August 1979.

118. Mulroe, *Bombs, Bullets and the Border*, p. 213.

119. *Irish Press*, 9 July and 15 October 1980.

120. Ibid. See also Ó Faoleán, *A Broad Church*, pp. 158–61.

121. Hanley, *The Impact of the Troubles*, pp. 68–116; Kissane, 'Defending Democracy?', pp. 171–2.

122. Enda Dooley, *Homicide in Ireland, 1972–1991* (Dublin: The Stationery Office, 1995). Whether the wider climate of political instability created the conditions for a more general increase in homicide rates is, however, worthy of further investigation. Randolph Roth, *American Homicide* (Cambridge, MA: Harvard University Press, 2009). Loyalist paramilitaries were responsible for almost 50 murders during the 1970s, 33 of them in the Dublin and Monaghan bombings of May 1974.

123. Brendan O'Brien, *The Long War: The IRA and Sinn Féin* (Dublin: The O'Brien Press, 1999), pp. 121, 161.

124. The IRA had carried out the abduction and murder of German businessman Thomas Niedermayer in Belfast in 1973, but that had been done in the hope of exchanging the victim for republican prisoners, rather than for ransom. Chris Thornton, Seamus Kelters, Brian Feeney and David McKittrick, *Lost Lives: The stories of the men, women and children who died as a result of the Northern Ireland Troubles* (Edinburgh: Mainstream Publishing, 1999), pp. 410–11. Breakaway groups had also utilised this tactic in the 1970s. See Hanley, *The Impact of the Troubles*, p. 54.

125. Paul Howard, *Hostage: Notorious Irish kidnappings* (Dublin: The O'Brien Press, 2004), pp. 185–214.

126. Ed Moloney, *A Secret History of the IRA* (London: Penguin Allen Lane, 2002), pp. 242, 262.

127. *The Irish Times*, 8 August 1983.

128. *An Phoblacht/Republican News*, 21 December 1983.

129. *Irish Press*, 27 February 1982. The INLA claimed that the group involved were 'rejects' and that it did not target gardaí.

130. *Irish Independent*, 24 August 1984.

131. *Cork Examiner*, 28 June 1985.

132. *Irish Press*, 28 November 1987.

133. *Irish Independent*, 7 May 1988.

134. Ibid., 13 January 1990.

135. *Irish Press*, 18 January 1990.

136. *Hansard*, vol. 165, CC 632–3W, 23 January 1990.

137. *Irish Independent*, 28 January 1990.

138. *Cork Examiner*, 7 July 1990.

139. Moloney, *A Secret History of the IRA*, pp. 1–33.

140. *The Irish Times*, 8 January 1992.

141. Ibid., 9 May 1990.

142. The IRA's rank and file were led to believe that some operations, particularly robberies, would continue despite the ceasefire. Tommy McKearney, *The Provisional IRA: From insurrection to parliament* (London: Pluto Press, 2011), p. 179.

143. *Irish Independent*, 8 June 1996; Richard English, *Armed Struggle: A history of the IRA* (London: Macmillan, 2003), p. 291; *An Phoblacht/Republican News*, 21 December 2000.

144. Ó Faoleán, *A Broad Church*, p. 119.

CHAPTER 4: BLURRING OF BOUNDARIES?

1. See, for example, report on the Official IRA's activities in Lurgan in *United Irishman*, March 1972.

2. *The Irish Times*, 20 August 1981.

3. English, *Armed Struggle*, p. 275.

4. Belfastman Hugh O'Halloran died after an Official IRA punishment beating supposedly carried out with hurleys in September 1979. Chris Thornton, Seamus Kelters, Brian Feeney and David McKittrick, *Lost Lives: The stories of the men, women and children who died as a result of the Northern Ireland Troubles* (Edinburgh: Mainstream Publishing, 1999), p. 800.

5. *An Phoblacht/Republican News*, 25 July 1982.

6. *The Irish Times*, 30 July 1980.

7. John D. Brewer, Bill Lockhart and Paula Rodgers, 'Informal Social Control and Crime Management in Belfast', *The British Journal of Sociology*, vol. 49, 1998, pp. 570–85.

8. Anne Cadwallader, 'IRA-Style Crime and Punishment', *Fortnight*, no. 209, November 1984, pp. 8–10.

9. Republican activist Patrick Magee describes how the 'hoods' emerged in the mid-1970s and how 'grievance and disaffection' from 'teens in particular' had made the environment in nationalist areas more difficult for the IRA. Patrick Magee, *Building Bridges after the Brighton Bomb: Where grieving begins. A memoir* (London: Pluto Press, 2021), p. 85.

10. *An Phoblacht/Republican News*, 12 November 1981.

11. Ciarán de Baróid, *Ballymurphy and the Irish War* (London: Pluto Press, 1990), pp. xv–xvi.

12. Ian Cobain, *Anatomy of a Killing: Life and death on a divided island* (London: Granta, 2020), pp. 166–7.

13. Ronnie Munck, 'Repression, Insurgency and Popular Justice: The Irish case', *Crime and Social Justice*, nos 21/2, 1984, pp. 81–94.

14. *The Independent*, 20 December 1992.

15. Eamonn McCann, *War and an Irish Town* (London: Pluto Press, 1993), pp. 20–3.

16. *Irish Examiner*, 19 October 2014.

17. For a variety of views on kneecapping and IRA policing see Fionnuala O'Connor, *In Search of a State: Catholics in Northern Ireland* (Belfast: The Blackstaff Press, 1993), pp. 127–31.

18. Bean, *The New Politics of Sinn Féin*, pp. 110–11.

19. Cadwallader, 'IRA-Style Crime and Punishment'.

20. John O'Farrell, 'Rough "Justice"', *Fortnight*, no. 376, February 1999, p. 8.

21. Suzanne Breen, 'Long War Over', *Fortnight*, no. 373, September 1998, p. 7; Suzanne Breen, 'A Tale of Two Murders', *Village*, 8 March 2005.

22. *Republican News*, 7 and 15 November 1975.

23. *The Irish Times*, 14 November 1975.

24. Ibid., 25 September 1984.

25. P.K. Clare, *Racketeering in Northern Ireland: A new version of the patriot game* (Chicago: University of Illinois Press, 1989).

26. John Mooney, *Gangster: The biography of international drug trafficker John Gilligan* (Dublin: Maverick House, 2011), p. 64.

27. John Mooney and Michael O'Toole, *Black Operations: The secret war against the Real IRA* (Dublin: Maverick House, 2003), pp. 54–9.

28. Ó Faoleán, *A Broad Church*, p. 119.

29. Sam McGrath, 'Gangland Murders in Dublin', *Come Here to Me*, 17 April 2020.

30. Jack Holland, *The American Connection: U.S. money, guns and influence in Northern Ireland* (Dublin: Poolbeg Press, 1989), pp. 71, 88–90.

31. Patrick Nee, *A Criminal and an Irishman: The inside story of the Boston mob – IRA connection* (Hanover: Steerforth, 2007).

32. Dick Lehr and Gerard O'Neill, *Whitey: The life of America's most notorious mob boss* (London: Ebury, 2015), pp. 256–8.

33. *Sinn Féin: Who Are They?*, TV3/Virgin Media, 2 December 2013.

34. Kevin Cullen and Shelley Murphy, *Whitey Bulger: America's most wanted gangster and the manhunt that brought him to justice* (New York: Norton, 2013); *Irish Examiner*, 9 September 2006.

35. Sam Millar, *On the Brinks* (Dublin: The O'Brien Press, 2014); *The Irish Times*, 24 September 1993.

36. English, *Armed Struggle*, pp. 331–2.

37. *Irish Press*, 26 March 1990.

38. Jack Holland and Henry McDonald, *INLA: Deadly divisions* (Dublin: Torc, 1994), pp. 313–17.

39. *The Irish Times*, 7 November 1992; *Cork Examiner*, 2 November 1992.

40. Holland and McDonald, *Deadly Divisions*, pp. 341–3.

41. Jason O'Toole, 'Inside the IRA', *Hot Press*, 1 February 2007.

42. Gearóid Phelan, '"The Big Bluff" or the Double Bluff? The Concerned Parents Against Drugs and the Provisional IRA', *History Studies*, vol. 11, 2010, pp. 74–5.

43. *Inner-City Republican*, November 1983.

44. *Irish Press*, 4 October 1982; Phelan, '"The Big Bluff"', p. 71.

45. John Noonan, *What Do I Do Now?* (Dublin: J.N. Print, 2005), pp. 117–34.

46. Scott Millar, '"The Risen People": Sinn Féin development in Dublin 1981–2002', MA thesis, Dublin City University, 2002, pp. 5–6.

47. André Lyder, *Pushers Out: The inside story of Dublin's anti-drugs movement* (Dublin: Trafford, 2005), pp. 35–54.

48. The Coalition of Communities Against Drugs.

49. Lyder, *Pushers Out*, pp. 290–2.

50. Thornton, Kelters, Feeney and McKittrick, *Lost Lives*, pp. 1377–8; Mooney, *Gangster*, pp. 115–19.

51. Matt Treacy, *A Tunnel to the Moon: The end of the Irish Republican Army* (Dublin: Brocaire Books, 2017), p. 92.

52. Moloney, *A Secret History of the IRA*, pp. 437–40.

53. *The Irish Times*, 6 June 1997.

54. Ibid., 15 October 1999.

55. *Irish Examiner*, 9 October 2002.

56. Mooney, *Gangster*, pp. 113–15.

57. Mooney and O'Toole, *Black Operations*, pp. 85–91.

58. Bean, *The New Politics of Sinn Féin*, pp. 93–4.

59. Ibid., p. 108.

60. Anon. in Sean O'Mahoney Papers, 2005, National Library of Ireland, MS 44,301/5.

61. For a fictional account of a similar robbery see Richard O'Rawe, *Northern Heist* (Newbridge: Merrion Press, 2018).

62. Anthony McIntyre, *Good Friday: The death of Irish republicanism* (New York: Ausubo, 2008), pp. 157–74, 251–65.

63. For a nuanced account of the traditions of republicanism in south Armagh see Patrick Mulroe, 'Moving Away from the "Bandit Country" Myth', in Neil Fleming and James H. Murphy (eds), *Ireland and Partition: Contexts and consequences* (Clemson, SC: Clemson University Press, 2021).

64. Thomas Leahy, *The Intelligence War Against the IRA* (Cambridge: Cambridge University Press, 2020), pp. 172–3.

65. *An Phoblacht/Republican News*, 20 March 2003; *The Irish Times*, 14 March 2003.

66. 'Glory is Tarnished as Idealism is Eroded', *Fourthwrite*, Winter, 2007, pp. 6–9.

67. *The Irish Times*, 24 December 2015 and 26 February 2016.

68. Ibid., 10 January 2019.

69. Ibid., 9 November 2019.

70. *The Irish Times*, 20 October 2015. See also *Sunday World*, 2 August 2021.

71. Between 1998 and 2007 only 16 of the 449 prisoners released had their licences revoked. Democratic Progress Institute, *The Good Friday Agreement: Prisoner release processes* (London: Democratic Progress Institute, 2013), pp. 14–15.

72. 'Criminality of Micro Groups Exposed', *An Phoblacht*, 5 February 2009.

73. Ibid., 27 August 2010.

74. *Derry Journal*, 26 February 2010. RAAD has since become part of the 'New IRA.'

75. Martyn Frampton, *Legion of the Rearguard: Dissident Irish republicanism* (Dublin: Irish Academic Press, 2011), pp. 260–3.

76. Marisa McGlinchey, *Unfinished Business: The politics of 'dissident' Irish republicanism* (Manchester: Manchester University Press, 2019), pp. 162–5.

77. *The Irish Times*, 12 April 2018; *Irish News*, 5 December 2019.

78. In April 2022 one of the armed groups, Óglaigh na hÉireann, claimed to have recently taken 'lethal action' against drug dealers. *The Journal*, 19 April 2022.

79. *Irish Sun*, 7 February 2020.

80. Donnchadh Ó Laoghaire, TD, 'Sinn Féin Submission to the Commission on the Future of Policing' (Dublin: Sinn Féin, 2018); *Irish Sun*, 7 February 2020.

81. *The Irish Times*, 30 October 2021.

EPILOGUE

1. Stephen Breen and Owen Conlon, *The Cartel: The shocking true story of the rise of the Kinahan crime cartel and its deadly feud with the Hutch gang* (Dublin: Penguin Ireland, 2017).

2. *Irish Independent*, 27 April 2021.

3. *The Sun*, 23 April 2016; *Irish Independent* and *Belfast Telegraph*, 23 May 2016.

4. *Irish News*, 29 June 2020.

5. Aogán Mulcahy, 'The Impact of the Northern "Troubles" on Criminal Justice in the Irish Republic', in Paul O'Mahony

(ed.), *Criminal Justice in Ireland* (Dublin: Institute of Public Administration, 2002), pp. 281–3.

6. Niamh Hourigan, 'Organised Crime and Community Violence: Understanding Limerick's "regimes of fear"', in Niamh Hourigan (ed.), *Understanding Limerick: Social exclusion and change* (Cork: Cork University Press, 2011), pp. 74–102.

7. Mulcahy, 'The Impact of the Northern "Troubles"'.

8. Mooney and O'Toole, *Black Operations*, p. 302.

9. *Saoirse – Irish Freedom*, October 2012.

10. *Sunday Tribune*, 8 March 2009.

11. *Saoirse Nua*, (N/D) 2017.

12. Michael Hall, (ed.), *Republicanism in Transition: (2) Beginning the debate* (Newtownabbey: Island Pamphlets, 2011), pp. 17–26.

13. Antaine Mac Dhomhnaill, 'The Republican Position After Good Friday', *The Pensive Quill*, 1 January 2014.

14. See also Niamh Hourigan, John F. Morrison, James Windle and Andrew Silke, 'Crime in Ireland North and South: Feuding gangs and profiteering paramilitaries', *Trends in Organized Crime*, vol. 21, no. 2, 2018, pp. 126–46.

Bibliography

NEWSPAPERS
Anglo-Celt
An Phoblacht
An Phoblacht/Republican News
An t-Óglách
Belfast News Letter
Belfast Telegraph
Connacht Tribune
Cork Examiner
Daily Telegraph
Derry Journal
Donegal News
Éire
Evening Herald
Evening Press
Freeman's Journal
Fortnight
Fourthwrite
Hansard
Hibernia
Inner-City Republican
Irish Bulletin
Irish Examiner
Irish Independent
Irish News
Irish Press
Killarney Echo and South Kerry Chronicle
Leinster Express
Leitrim Observer
Limerick Leader
Magill
Munster Express

Nationalist and Leinster Times
Old Ireland
Republican News
Saoirse – Irish Freedom
Saoirse Nua
Sligo Champion
Strabane Chronicle
Sunday Independent
Sunday Press
Sunday Tribune
Sunday World
The Guardian
The Kerryman
The Independent
The Irish Sun
The Irish Times
The Journal
The Nation
The Pensive Quill
This Week
Tipperary Star
Tuam Herald
United Irishman
Wicklow Newsletter
Workers' Republic

THESES

McGuill, Paul, 'Political Violence in the Republic of Ireland 1969–1997', MA thesis, University College Dublin, 1998

Millar, Scott, '"The Risen People": Sinn Féin development in Dublin 1981–2002', MA thesis, Dublin City University, 2002

Murphy, Breen, 'The Government's Executions Policy during the Irish Civil War 1922–23', PhD thesis, NUI Maynooth, 2010

BOOKS AND ARTICLES

Abbot, Richard, *Police Casualties in Ireland, 1919–1922* (Cork: Mercier Press, 2000)

Barrett, J.J., *Martin Ferris: Man of Kerry* (Dingle: Brandon, 2005)

Bean, Kevin, *The New Politics of Sinn Féin* (Liverpool: Liverpool University Press, 2007)

Borgonovo, John, 'Republican Courts, Ordinary Crime, and the Irish Revolution, 1919–21', in M. de Koster, H. Leuwers, D. Luyten and X. Rousseaux (eds), *Justice in Wartime and Revolutions: Europe, 1795–1950* (Brussels: Archives Generals du Royame, 2012)

——, *The Battle for Cork: July–August 1922* (Cork: Mercier Press, 2011)

Bowyer Bell, J., *IRA Tactics and Targets* (Dublin: Poolbeg Press, 1990)

——, *The Secret Army: The IRA from 1916* (Dublin: The Academy Press, 1979)

Breathnach, Aoife, *Becoming Conspicuous: Irish Travellers, society and the state, 1922–70* (Dublin: UCD Press, 2006)

Breen, Stephen and Owen Conlon, *The Cartel: The shocking true story of the rise of the Kinahan crime cartel and its deadly feud with the Hutch gang* (Dublin: Penguin Ireland, 2017)

Breen, Suzanne, 'A Tale of Two Murders', *Village*, 8 March 2005

——, 'Long War Over', *Fortnight*, no. 373, September 1998

Brennan, Joe, *Superdollar: A North Korean conspiracy* (Belfast: OJM, 2011)

Brewer, John D., Bill Lockhart and Paula Rodgers, 'Informal Social Control and Crime Management in Belfast', *The British Journal of Sociology*, vol. 49, 1998

Burke, Edward, *An Army of Tribes: British army cohesion, deviancy and murder in Northern Ireland* (Liverpool: Liverpool University Press, 2018)

Earner-Byrne, Lindsey, 'The Rape of Mary M: A microhistory of sexual violence and moral redemption in 1920's Ireland', *Journal of the History of Sexuality*, vol. 24, no. 1, January 2015

Cadwallader, Anne, 'IRA-Style Crime and Punishment', *Fortnight*, no. 209, November 1984

Campbell, Brian, Laurence McKeown and Felim O'Hagan (eds), *Nor Meekly Serve My Time: The H-Block struggle 1976–1981* (Belfast: Beyond the Pale, 1994)

Clare, P.K., *Racketeering in Northern Ireland: A new version of the patriot game* (Chicago: University of Illinois Press, 1989)

Clark, Gemma, 'Violence against Women in the Irish Civil War, 1922–3: Gender-based harm in global perspective', *Irish Historical Studies*, vol. 44, no. 165, 2020

Cobain, Ian, *Anatomy of a Killing: Life and death on a divided island* (London: Granta, 2020)

Coleman, Marie, 'Violence against Women in the Irish War of Independence, 1919–1921', in Diarmaid Ferriter and Susannah Riordan (eds), *Years of Turbulence: The Irish revolution and its aftermath* (Dublin: UCD Press, 2015)

——, *County Longford and the Irish Revolution, 1910–1923* (Dublin: Irish Academic Press, 2003)

Connolly, Linda, 'Sexual Violence in the Irish Civil War: A forgotten war crime?', *Women's History Review*, 2020

——, 'Towards a Further Understanding of the Sexual and Gender-based Violence Women Experienced in the Irish Revolution', in Linda Connolly (ed.), *Women and the Irish Revolution* (Newbridge: Irish Academic Press, 2020)

Conway, Kieran, *Southside Provisional: From freedom fighter to the Four Courts* (Dublin: Orpen Press, 2014)

Conway, Vicky, *Policing Independent Ireland: A history of An Garda Síochána* (London: Routledge, 2013)

Cronin, Sean, *Irish Nationalism: A history of its roots and ideology* (Dublin: The Academy Press, 1980)

Cullen, Kevin and Shelley Murphy, *Whitey Bulger: America's most wanted gangster and the manhunt that brought him to justice* (New York: Norton, 2013) de Baróid, Ciarán, *Ballymurphy and the Irish War* (London: Pluto Press, 1990)

Democratic Progress Institute, *The Good Friday Agreement: Prisoner release processes* (London: Democratic Progress Institute, 2013)

Department of Justice, *Homicide in Ireland, 1972–1991* (Dublin: The Stationery Office, 1995)

Dolan, Anne and C.H. O'Malley (eds), *'No Surrender Here!' The Civil War papers of Ernie O'Malley 1922–24* (Dublin: The Lilliput Press, 2007)

Dooley, Enda, *Homicide in Ireland, 1972–1991* (Dublin: The Stationery Office, 1995).

Dooley, Terence, *Monaghan: The Irish revolution, 1912–23* (Dublin: Four Courts Press, 2017)

Dorney, John, *The Civil War in Dublin: The fight for the Irish capital 1922–24* (Newbridge: Merrion Press, 2017)

Doyle, David M. and Liam O'Callaghan, *Capital Punishment in Independent Ireland: A social, legal and political history* (Liverpool: Liverpool University Press, 2019)

Dungan, Myles, *Four Killings: Land hunger, murder and a family in the Irish revolution* (London: Head of Zeus, 2021)

Dunne, Derek, 'A very Special Criminal Court', *Magill*, 15 May 1985

—— and Gene Kerrigan, *Round Up the Usual Suspects: The Cosgrave coalition and Nicky Kelly* (Dublin: Gill & Macmillan, 1984)

Dunne, Terry, 'The Agrarian Movement of 1920: Cattle drivers, marauders, terrorists and hooligans', *History Ireland*, vol. 28, 2020

English, Richard, *Armed Struggle: A history of the IRA* (London: Macmillan, 2003)

Fallon, Donal, 'Newsboys and the "Animal Gang" in 1930s Dublin', in David Convery (ed), *Locked Out: A century of Irish working-class life* (Dublin: Irish Academic Press, 2013)

Earls FitzGerald, Thomas, *Combatants and Civilians in Revolutionary Ireland, 1918–1923* (London: Routledge, 2021)

Flynn, Sean and Pádraig Yeates, *Smack! The criminal drugs racket in Ireland* (Dublin: Gill & Macmillan, 1985)

Foster, Gavin M., *The Irish Civil War and Society: Politics, class and conflict* (Basingstoke: Palgrave Macmillan, 2015)

Foy, Michael, *The Aftermath of Revolution: Sligo 1921–23* (Dublin: UCD Press, 2000)

Frampton, Martyn, *Legion of the Rearguard: Dissident Irish republicanism* (Dublin: Irish Academic Press, 2011)

Glennon, Kieran, *From Pogrom to Civil War: Tom Glennon and the Belfast IRA* (Cork: Mercier Press, 2013)

Gormally, Brian, 'From Punishment to Restorative Justice in Northern Ireland', *Accord: An international review of peace initiatives*, 2015

Grant, Adrian, *Derry: The Irish revolution, 1912–23* (Dublin: Four Courts Press, 2018).

Great Britain: Parliament: House of Commons: Northern Ireland Affairs: 'Organised Crime in Northern Ireland' (London: Westminster, 2005)

O'Sullivan Greene, Patrick, *Crowdfunding the Revolution: The First Dáil Loan and the battle for Irish independence* (Dublin: Eastwood, 2020)

Hall, Michael (ed.), *Republicanism in Transition: (2) Beginning the debate* (Newtownabbey: Island Pamphlets, 2011)

Hanley, Brian, '"The Irish and the Jews Have a Good Deal in Common": Irish republicanism, anti-Semitism and the post-war world', *Irish Historical Studies*, vol. 44, no. 165, May 2020

——, *The Impact of the Troubles on the Republic of Ireland, 1968–79* (Manchester: Manchester University Press, 2018)

——, '"The Layers of an Onion": Reflections on 1913, class and the memory of the Irish revolution', in Conor McNamara and Pádraig Yeates (eds), *The Dublin Lockout 1913: New perspectives on class war & its legacy* (Dublin: Irish Academic Press, 2017)

——, '"The Needs of the People": The IRA considers its future, 1967–68', *Saothar*, vol. 38, 2013

——, *The IRA: A documentary history 1916–2005* (Dublin: Gill & Macmillan, 2010)

—— and Scott Millar, *The Lost Revolution: The story of the Official IRA and the Workers' Party* (Dublin: Penguin Ireland, 2009)

——, *The IRA 1926–1936* (Dublin: Four Courts Press, 2002)

Hart, Peter, *The IRA and Its Enemies: Violence and community in Cork 1916–1923* (Oxford: Oxford University Press, 1998)

Healy, Michael, *Saor Éire: The unfinished revolution. The struggle for a socialist republic, 1967–73* (Kildare: Irish Republican and Marxist History Project, 2021)

Hobsbawm, Eric, *Bandits* (London: Abacus, 2001)

Holland, Jack, *The American Connection: U.S. money, guns and influence in Northern Ireland* (Dublin: Poolbeg Press, 1989)

—— and Henry McDonald, *INLA: Deadly divisions* (Dublin: Torc, 1994)

Hopkinson, Michael, *Green Against Green: The Irish Civil War* (Dublin: Gill & Macmillan, 1989)

Hourigan, Niamh, John F. Morrison, James Windle and Andrew Silke, 'Crime in Ireland North and South: Feuding gangs and profiteering paramilitaries', *Trends in Organized Crime*, vol. 21, no. 2, 2018, pp. 126–46

Hourigan, Niamh, 'Organised Crime and Community Violence: Understanding Limerick's "regimes of fear"', in Niamh Hourigan (ed.), *Understanding Limerick: Social exclusion and change* (Cork: Cork University Press, 2011)

Howard, Paul, *Hostage: Notorious Irish kidnappings* (Dublin: The O'Brien Press, 2004)

Hughes, Brendan and Douglas Dalby, *Up Like a Bird: The rise and fall of an IRA commander* (Castleisland: Time Warp Books, 2021)

Hughes, Brian, *Defying the IRA? Intimidation, coercion, and communities during the Irish revolution* (Liverpool: Liverpool University Press, 2016)

Irish Republican Socialist Party, *The History of the Irish Republican Socialist Movement. Volume 1: 1974–1979* (Belfast: IRSP, 2020)

——, *Framed through the Special Criminal Court: The 'great train robbery' trial* (Dublin: Starry Plough Publications, 1979)

Joy, Sinéad, *The IRA in Kerry 1916–1921* (Dublin: The Collins Press, 2005)

Keane, Michael, 'Dependency Claims for the Civil War Executed in the Military Service (1916–1923) Pensions Collection', *History Ireland*, vol. 26, March/April 2018

Kennedy, Liam, 'They Shoot Children, Don't They? An analysis of the age and gender of the victims of punishment attacks in Northern Ireland', report to the Northern Ireland Committee Against Terror and the House of Commons Northern Ireland Affairs Committee, 2001

Kerrigan, Gene, *Hard Cases: True stories of Irish crime* (Dublin: Gill & Macmillan, 1996)

Kissane, Bill, 'Defending Democracy? The legislative response to political extremism in the Irish Free State, 1922–39', *Irish Historical Studies*, vol. 34, no. 134, November 2004

Knox, Colin, 'From the Margins to the Mainstream: Community restorative justice in Northern Ireland', *Journal of Peacebuilding & Development*, vol. 8, no. 2, August 2013

Laffan, Michael, *The Resurrection of Ireland: The Sinn Féin party 1916–1923* (Cambridge: Cambridge University Press, 2005)

Leahy, Thomas, *The Intelligence War against the IRA* (Cambridge: Cambridge University Press, 2020)

Leeson, D.M., *The Black and Tans: British police and Auxiliaries in the Irish War of Independence, 1920–1921* (Oxford: Oxford University Press, 2011)

Lehr, Dick and Gerard O'Neill, *Whitey: The life of America's most notorious mob boss* (London: Ebury, 2015)

Lyder, André, *Pushers Out: The inside story of Dublin's anti-drugs movement* (Dublin: Trafford, 2005)

Lynch, Robert, 'Explaining the Altnaveigh Massacre', *Éire-Ireland*, fall/winter 2010

Luddy, Maria, *Prostitution and Irish Society, 1800–1940* (Cambridge: Cambridge University Press, 2007)

MacEoin, Uinseann, *The IRA in the Twilight Years, 1923–1948* (Dublin: Argenta, 1997)

Mac Suibhne, Breandán, 'The Generation that Lost: The Ulster Bank, Ardara, County Donegal, 16 June 1921, and long after, and far away', in Patrick Mannion and Fearghal McGarry (eds), *A Global History of Irish Revolution* (New York: New York University Press, 2022)

McCann, Eamonn, *War and an Irish Town* (London: Pluto Press, 1993)

McCarthy, Brian, *The Civic Guard Mutiny* (Cork: Mercier Press, 2012)

McCarthy, Pat, *The Irish Revolution: Waterford 1912–23* (Dublin: Four Courts Press, 2015)

McGlinchey, Marisa, *Unfinished Business: The politics of 'dissident' Irish republicanism* (Manchester: Manchester University Press, 2019)

McIntyre, Anthony, *Good Friday: The death of Irish republicanism* (New York: Ausubo, 2008)

McKearney, Tommy, *The Provisional IRA: From insurrection to parliament* (London: Pluto Press, 2011)

McLoughlin, Barry, *Left to the Wolves: Irish victims of Stalinist terror* (Dublin: Irish Academic Press, 2007)

—— and Emmet O'Connor, *In Spanish Trenches: The minds and deeds of the Irish who fought for the Spanish republic in the Spanish Civil War* (Dublin: UCD Press, 2020)

McNamara, Conor, *War and Revolution in the West of Ireland: Galway, 1913–1922* (Newbridge: Irish Academic Press, 2018)

McNulty, Thomas, *Exiled: 40 years an exile* (Monaghan: TMN Publications, 2013)

Magee, Patrick, *Building Bridges after the Brighton Bomb: Where grieving begins. A memoir* (London: Pluto Press, 2021)

——, *Gangsters or Guerrillas? Representations of Irish republicans in Troubles fiction* (Belfast: Beyond the Pale, 2001)

Mahon, Tom and James J. Gillogly, *Decoding the IRA* (Cork: Mercier Press, 2008)

Matthews, Ann, *Renegades: Irish republican women 1900–1922* (Cork: Mercier Press, 2010)

Millar, Sam, *On the Brinks* (Dublin: The O'Brien Press, 2014)

Mitchell, Arthur, *Revolutionary Government in Ireland: Dáil Éireann 1919–1922* (Dublin: Gill & Macmillan, 1995)

Moloney, Ed, *A Secret History of the IRA* (London: Penguin Allen Lane, 2002)

Mooney, John, *Gangster: The biography of international drug trafficker John Gilligan* (Dublin: Maverick House, 2011)

—— and Michael O'Toole, *Black Operations: The secret war against the Real IRA* (Dublin: Maverick House, 2003)

Moroney, Michael, *George Plant and the Rule of Law: The Devereux affair 1940–42* (Tipperary: County Tipperary Historical Society, 1989)

Morton, James, *East End Gangland* (London: Sphere, 2000)

Mulcahy, Aogán, 'The Impact of the Northern "Troubles" on Criminal Justice in the Irish Republic', in Paul O'Mahony (ed.), *Criminal Justice in Ireland* (Dublin: Institute of Public Administration, 2002)

Mulroe, Patrick, 'Moving Away from the "Bandit Country" Myth', in Neil Fleming and James H. Murphy (eds), *Ireland and Partition: Contexts and consequences* (Clemson, SC: Clemson University Press, 2021)

——, *Bombs, Bullets and the Border: Policing Ireland's frontier. Irish security policy, 1969–1978* (Newbridge: Irish Academic Press, 2017)

Munck, Ronnie, 'Repression, Insurgency and Popular Justice: The Irish case', *Crime and Social Justice*, nos 21–2, 1984

Nee, Patrick, *A Criminal and an Irishman: The inside story of the Boston mob – IRA connection* (Hanover: Steerforth, 2007)

Noonan, Gerard, *The IRA in Britain, 1919–1923: 'In the heart of enemy lines'* (Liverpool: Liverpool University Press, 2014)

Noonan, John, *What Do I Do Now?* (Dublin: J.N. Print, 2005)

O'Brien, Brendan, *The Long War: The IRA and Sinn Féin* (Dublin: The O'Brien Press, 1999)

O'Brien, Gerard, *An Garda Síochána and the Scott Medal* (Dublin: Four Courts Press, 2008)

O'Callaghan, John, *Limerick: The Irish revolution 1912–23* (Dublin: Four Courts Press, 2018)

O'Connor, Emmet, *A Labour History of Ireland 1824–2000* (Dublin: UCD Press, 2011)

O'Connor, Fionnuala, *In Search of a State: Catholics in Northern Ireland* (Belfast: The Blackstaff Press, 1993)

O'Donoghue, David, *The Devil's Deal: The IRA, Nazi Germany and the double life of Jim O'Donovan* (Dublin: New Island, 2010)

Ó Drisceoil, Donal, 'Storm Centre: The Brigade Activity Reports from Cork', in *The Military Service (1916–1923) Pensions Collection: The Brigade Activity Reports* (Dublin: The Military Archives, 2018)

Ó Faoleán, Gearóid, *A Broad Church: The Provisional IRA in the Republic of Ireland 1969–1980* (Newbridge: Merrion Press, 2019)

O'Farrell, John, 'Rough "Justice"', *Fortnight*, no. 376, February 1999

O'Halpin, Eunan, 'Counting Terror: Bloody Sunday and the dead of the Irish revolution', in David Fitzpatrick (ed.), *Terror in Ireland, 1916–1923* (Dublin: The Lilliput Press, 2012)

O'Hearn, Denis, *Nothing But an Unfinished Song: Bobby Sands, the hunger striker who ignited a generation* (New York: Nation Books, 2006)

O'Leary, Brendan, 'Mission Accomplished? Looking back at the IRA', *Field Day Review*, vol. 1, 2005

O'Malley, Cormac and Vincent Keane (eds), *The Men Will Talk to Me: Mayo interviews by Ernie O'Malley* (Cork: Mercier Press, 2014)

O'Rawe, Richard, *Northern Heist* (Newbridge: Merrion Press, 2018)

———, *Blanketmen: An untold story of the H-Block hunger strike* (Dublin: New Island, 2005)

Ó Ruairc, Pádraig Óg, *Truce: Murder, myth and the last days of the Irish War of Independence* (Cork: Mercier Press, 2016)

O'Toole, Jason, 'Inside the IRA', *Hot Press*, 1 February 2007

Phelan, Gearóid, '"The Big Bluff" or the Double Bluff? The Concerned Parents Against Drugs and the Provisional IRA', *History Studies*, vol. 11, 2010

Phelan, Jim, *The Name's Phelan: The first autobiography of Jim Phelan* (Newtownards: Blackstaff Press, 1993)

Radden Keefe, Patrick, *Say Nothing: A true story of murder and memory in Northern Ireland* (London: William Collins, 2019)

Regan, John M., *The Irish Counter-Revolution 1921–1936* (Dublin: Gill & Macmillan, 1999)

Republican Movement, *Tírghrá: Ireland's patriot dead* (Dublin: National Commemoration Committee, 2002)

Roth, Randolph, *American Homicide* (Cambridge, MA: Harvard University Press, 2009)

Shore, Heather, *London's Criminal Underworlds c. 1720 – c. 1930* (London: Palgrave, 2015)

Thornton, Chris, Seamus Kelters, Brian Feeney and David McKittrick, *Lost Lives: The stories of the men, women and children who died as a result of the Northern Ireland Troubles* (Edinburgh: Mainstream Publishing, 1999)

Townshend, Charles, *The Republic: The fight for Irish independence* (London: Penguin, 2014)

Treacy, Matt, *A Tunnel to the Moon: The end of the Irish Republican Army* (Dublin: Brocaire Books, 2017)

Williams, Paul, *Badfellas* (Dublin: Penguin Ireland, 2011)

Wilson, T.K., *Frontiers of Violence: Conflict and identity in Ulster and Upper Silesia 1918–1922* (Oxford: Oxford Historical Monographs, 2010)

Yeates, Pádraig, *A City in Turmoil: Dublin 1919–21* (Dublin: Gill & Macmillan, 2015)

——, 'Who Were Dublin's Looters in 1916? Crime and society in Dublin during the Great War', *Saothar,* vol. 41, 2016

ONLINE ARTICLES

Dorney, John, 'The Tragedies of Ballyconnell', *The Irish Story*, 19 June 2014

——, 'Policing Revolutionary Dublin', *The Irish Story*, 21 June 2016

Glennon, Kieran, 'Belfast Republicans and the Treaty Split of 1922', *The Irish Story*, 26 March 2022

Mac Dhomhnaill, Antaine, 'The Republican Position After Good Friday', *The Pensive Quill*, 1 January 2014

McGrath, Sam, 'Gangland Murders in Dublin', *Come Here to Me*, 17 April 2020

——, 'Claude Gunner's Gang', *Come Here to Me*, 23 July 2018

——, 'The Sons of Dawn – Dublin's "Midnight Crawlers"', *Come Here to Me*, 12 September 2017

Military Service Pensions Blog, 'Killing Their Own – Philip Doyle and Jeremiah Gaffney', 14 November 2019

Mooney, Joe, 'A Family at War with the Empire: Christy and "Dina" Crothers of the Irish Citizen Army', *East Wall for All*, 4 April 2016.

Murray, Ciarán, 'The Bolsheviki Bookies', *Come Here to Me*, 29 March 2017

Whelan, Fergus, 'Street War', *Look Left*, 4 August 2012

DOCUMENTARIES

'The Man with the Hat': The revolutionary life and times of Sean Garland, Gansee Films, dir. Kevin Brannigan, 2018

A Mother Brings Her Son To Be Shot, Blinder Films, dir. Sinéad O'Shea, 2017

Sinn Féin: Who Are They?, TV3/Virgin Media, 2 December 2013

Index

Please note that St is treated as Saint and Mc is treated as Mac.

Abbeyfeale, County Limerick 39
Aiken, Frank 45
Air Raid Protection Service 64
Allied Irish Bank
  Belfast branch 76
  Grafton Street branch 76
  Lisduggan branch 86
'animal gangs' 61–2
Annaghdown, County Galway 48
An Phoblacht 5, 61–2
anti-treaty faction *see* Irish
  Republican Army
An t-Óglách 26, 32, 39
Ardee, County Louth 85
Ardee Hall, Talbot Street 62
Arklow, County Wicklow 18
Armagh town 38
arms *see* gun-running; Irish
  Republican Army
Athenry, County Galway 50
Athy, County Kildare 86

Ballaghaderreen, County
  Roscommon 27
Ballinamore, County Leitrim 54, 57,
  84, 85
Ballybofey, County Donegal 40
Ballyconnell, County Cavan 47
Ballymurphy, Belfast 91
Baltinglass, County Wicklow 68
Bank of Ireland 44
  Elphin branch 39
  Pembroke branch 29
  Tipperary branch 55
bank raids 14, 20, 26, 27, 28–9, 37,
  38, 39, 40, 44–5, 47, 50, 51,
  54, 55, 63, 64–5, 67–8, 69–70,
  71, 76–7, 82–3, 85, 86, 87

Barna Gap, County Limerick 79
Barnett, Ginger 30–1
Barr, Michael 109
Barrington, Gilbert 31
Bean, Kevin 93
Belfast, County Antrim 29, 40, 50,
  63, 64, 66, 69, 71, 76, 77, 79,
  80, 91, 92, 93–4, 95, 98, 104,
  107, 109
  inter-communal violence 69
Belfast Telegraph 107
Bell, Alan 26
Bergin, John 42
Biggs, Eileen 43
Birmingham 30, 31
Bishop, Michael 42
Black and Tans 25, 29, 37–8
'Black Hand' gang 24, 25, 37
Blessington, County Wicklow 51
Blueshirt movement 60
Boardwalk Empire 5
Bowyer Bell, J. 65
Boylan, Seán 21
Britain 14, 31, 32, 45
  arms purchased in 32
  bombing campaign in 62
  robberies authorised in 76
Brolly, Francie 5
Brown, Walter 15
Browne, Bernard 82, 83
Broy, Detective Eamon 12
Bryan, Martin 85
Buckley, Bridget 16
Buckley, Daniel 24
Bulger, James 'Whitey' 97
Buncrana, County Donegal 45
Bureau of Military History 8

Burke, Luke 47
Byrne, Henry 82

Cahill, Martin (The General) 100, 101
Campbell, Jimmy 93–4
Campbell, Patrick 103
Cannon, Bernard 48
Carey, Colm 90
Carr, Denis 30
Carrickmacross, County Monaghan 48
Carroll, John 29
Carty, Francis 19, 44
Casey, James 52
Castlebar, County Mayo 42
Castleblaney, County Monaghan 40
Castlepollard, County Westmeath 63
Ceannt, Áine 20
Charlestown, County Mayo 28, 41
Charleville, County Cork 13, 16
Chase Manhattan Bank, Shannon 76
China 66
Civic Guards 36–7
    enlistment of ex-RIC 37
Civil War 1, 36, 41, 42, 43–9, 55
Clarke, James 63
'Claude Gunner's gang' 38
Clinton, Mark 24–5
Clones, County Monaghan 29
Coalition of Communities Against Drugs (COCAD) 101
COCAD see Coalition of Communities Against Drugs
cocaine trade 3, 98, 109
Cohalan, Archbishop Daniel 21
Collett, John 92–3
Collins, Francis 102
Collins, Gerry 83
Collins, Michael 21, 27, 36, 40, 41
Colombia 97

Concerned Parents Against Drugs (CPAD) 99–101
Conroy, William 47
construction industry fraud 71–2
Continuity IRA 2, 111
Cookstown, County Tyrone 16
Cork city 23, 25, 40, 43
Cosgrave, Patrick 49
Costello, Seamus 70
counterfeiting 74
Cox, John 42
CPAD see Concerned Parents Against Drugs
Creeslough, County Donegal 48, 49
Criminal Assets Bureau 105
Croom, County Limerick 40
Crothers, Christy 51
Crowley, Patrick 54
Cull, Michael 47
Cullaville, County Armagh 104
Cumann na mBan 16, 43
Cumann na nGaedheal 60
Cunningham, James 31
Cunningham, Patrick 47
Cusack, Jim 2

DAAD see Direct Action Against Drugs
Dáil Éireann 23, 24, 26, 33
    inaugurated 12
    new legal system 14–15
Deignan, Annie 16
Delaney, James 30
de Meo, George 96
Dermody, Patrick 63
Derry city 106
Desmond, William 22
de Stacpoole, George, Duke 21
de Valera, Eamon 32, 51, 60, 61, 62
Devereux, Michael 56
Devine, Edward 40

Dillon, John 67
Direct Action Against Drugs (DAAD) 102
Donegal town 77–8, 82
Donnelly, Simon 15, 18, 33, 39, 41
Doon, County Limerick 48
Dowdall, Jonathan 109
Downes, William 52
Doyle, Archie 55, 65
Doyle, John 54
Doyle, Philip 50–1
Drew, James 18
Drogheda, County Louth 39
drug crime 1, 2–3, 4, 97–102, 106, 109, 111
Drumboe, County Donegal 48
Dublin 12, 13, 16, 18, 19, 21–2, 25, 27, 28, 29–30, 36, 37, 39, 48, 49, 50, 51–2, 63, 64–5, 67–8, 74, 76, 77, 78, 82, 84, 85, 86, 96, 99, 100, 102, 103, 105, 109, 111
   'animal gangs' 61–2
   drug problem 99–102, 109, 111
Dublin Castle 36
Dublin Metropolitan Police 13, 39, 48
Dublin Savings Bank, 29
Duffy, Colin 3
Dundalk, County Louth 54, 63
Dún Laoghaire, County Dublin 68
Dunleavy, Patrick 42
Dunleavy, Thomas 42
Dunne, Ben 84
Dunne, Christy 68

Easter Rising (1916) 12
Elphin, County Roscommon 39
Ennis, County Clare 26
Enniscorthy, County Wexford 86
Ennistymon, County Clare 27
Evening Herald 36

Fallon, Richard 68
FARC 98
Farrell, James 82
Fay's store, Edenderry, County Offaly 46
Feakle, County Clare 86
Feeney, Brian 95
Ferris, Martin 97
Fethard, County Tipperary 55
Fianna Fáil 60, 61
Fine Gael 60
Fishery Conservation Board 17
Fitzgerald, Seamus 25
Fitzgerald, Tom 51
Fletcher, Esther 45
Four Courts, Dublin 44
Free State army (National Army) 36, 41, 42, 43, 44, 45, 49, 52, 53, 85
   implicated in sexual violence 43
   receiving wages 44
Freyne, James 52

gangland disputes 96, 109
Garland, Seán 74
General Order No. 8 65, 66
Germany 62, 63
Glasgow 45
Glen of Aherlow, County Tipperary 49
Good, Joe 31
Good Friday Agreement 106
Gordon, William 24–5
Gorey, County Wexford 18
Goss, Richard 64
Goulding, Cathal 66, 67, 69
Graham, Peter 75
Grealy, Michael 47
Green, F.L.
   Odd Man Out 64
Green, Max 40

Gregory, Tony 99
Griffith, Jackie 65
gun-running 97

Haines, Joseph 64
Hamburg, Germany 31
Hand, Frank 85
Harrington, Seán 64
Harrison, George 96–7
H-Block protest 80, 84
Hehir, Hugh 86
Henderson, Frank 25
Hibernian Bank, Charlestown 41–2
Higgins, Austin 86
Hobsbawm, Eric 7
hunger strikes 6, 62, 84
Hutch crime family 109

ICA see Irish Citizen Army
Igoe, Bartley 45
Independent Monitoring
    Commission 4
INLA see Irish National Liberation
    Army
Innishannon, County Cork 18
internment 51, 62, 75
IPLO see Irish People's Liberation
    Organisation
IRA see Irish Republican Army
Irish Citizen Army (ICA) 15–16, 27,
    51, 52
Irish Independent 2
Irish National Liberation Army
    (INLA) 3, 4, 5, 78–9, 85, 92,
    96, 98, 102–3, 111
Irish People's Liberation
    Organisation (IPLO) 98
Irish Press, The 83
Irish Prison Board 40
Irish Republican Army (IRA)
    anti-treaty faction 36–51, 61
    arms dumps 95

arms supply for 27, 30–2, 70, 86,
    97
bombing campaign in Britain 62
border campaign 6, 65, 96
ceasefires 50, 53, 70, 72, 94, 101,
    102, 103
courts not recognised by 56
fundraising 8, 26–7, 45, 54–5,
    62–7, 69–71, 72–3, 74–6, 81–2,
    83, 84, 85, 87, 95
gangs posing as the 19
punishments by 15, 17, 18–19,
    20, 21, 24–5, 28, 37, 50–1, 80,
    90–5, 106
    of sex offenders 92–3
pro-treaty faction 36, 37, 43–5,
    49–50
release of prisoners 60
robberies authorised in Britain 76
splits in 36, 40–7, 69, 78, 103
treatment of 'tinkers' 22–3
veterans recruited into garda
    detective branch 61
wages 79
see also Continuity IRA; Irish
    Republican Police; Official
    Irish Republican Army;
    Provisional Irish Republican
    Army; Real IRA
Irish Republican Police (IRP) 15–16,
    18, 21, 27, 29, 32–3, 36,
    37–40, 42
    public order role 38–9
Irish Republican Socialist Party
    (IRSP) 78
Irish Times 37, 69, 94
IRP see Irish Republican Police
IRSP see Irish Republican Socialist
    Party

Kavanagh, Mary Ellen 45
Kearney, Andrew 94
Keenan, Brian 104
Kelleher, Denis 30

Kells, County Meath 29, 68
Kelly, Columb 47
Kelly, Eamon 3, 4, 74
Kelly, Patrick 85
Kennedy, Patrick 48
Keogh, John 53
Keogh, Patrick 56
Kerr, Frank 87
kidnappings 84–5
Kildare 37
Kilkenny town 39
Killakee House, Rathfarnham 40
Killarney, County Kerry 23
Killygordon, County Donegal 19
Kilmallock, County Limerick 40
Kinahan cartel 109
Kinsella, Joseph 18
kneecappings 1, 80, 90–2, 93, 100, 106, 107
'Knights of the Moon' 13
Knockvicar, County Roscommon 20

Lacey, Denis 49
Lahinch, County Clare 28
land disputes 23, 36, 50
Lanesborough, County Longford 42
Lavin, Thomas 23
Limerick 17, 20, 37
Littlejohn, Keith 76
Littlejohn, Kenneth 76
Liverpool 31, 53
London 30–1, 104
Long Good Friday, The 5
Longwood, County Meath 21
Love/Hate 1–2, 112
Lovelady, Thomas 53
Lybia 86
Lyder, André 101
Lynch, Liam 47
Lynch, Michael 26–7

McAllister, Jim 105
McAteer, Seán 52–3
McCabe, Jerry 87
McCartney, Robert 104
McCoy, John 38
McCullough, James 29
McDonagh, Nellie 48
McDonald, Geoffrey 24
McElroy, Patrick 64
Mac Giolla, Tomás 73
McGlichey, Patrick 19
McGrath, Joe 27
McGuinness, Cyril 105
McGurran, Malachy 67
McKenna, Arthur 91
McLaughlin, Ronan 103
McMullen, Felix 52
McNamee, Sean 94
Mac Stíofáin, Seán 75
McVicker, Alexander 91
Mafia 96
Maher, Kate 26
Martin, Hugh 53
Martin, Thomas J. 17
Maskey, Paul 106
Massey, Hugh Somerset, Lord 40
Millar, Sam 97
Miller alarms 53
Millstreet, County Cork 20, 24
Mitchell, William 29
Monaghan town 45
Monasterevin, County Kildare 19
money laundering 96
Monteagle, 2nd Baron of Brandon 21
Morley, John 82, 83
Morris, John 102
Morrissey, Patrick 85
Moylan, Seán 24, 41
Mulcahy, Paddy 67
Mulcahy, Richard 8, 21, 36

Mullingar, County Westmeath 16, 28, 46, 47
Murphy, Michael 50
Murphy, Robert 63
Murphy, Thomas 105
Murray, Kevin 109

National Army *see* Free State army
National Bank 29
neutrality 62
Newcestown, County Cork 16
New Ross, County Wexford 44
Newry 68, 87
NORAID 82
Northern Bank
    December 2004 robbery 103–4
    Oldcastle robbery 63
Northern Ireland 75, 81, 82, 83, 85, 87, 90, 94–5, 103, 106, 109
    Catholic refugees from 43
    civil war 50
    drug problem 102
    increasing violence in 1970s 75
    IRA border campaign 6, 65, 96

OASA *see* Offences Against the State Act
Ó Brádaigh, Ruairí 76
O'Brien, William 62
O'Callaghan, John 22
O'Connor, Jerome 82
O'Duffy, Eoin 51
Offences Against the State Act (OASA) 61, 77
Official Irish Republican Army (OIRA) 3, 69, 70–5, 76, 78, 82, 94–5
    ceasefire 70, 72
    construction industry fraud 71–2
    counterfeiting 74
    known as 'Group B' 72–3
    see also Irish Republican Army

O'Grady, John 3–4
O'Halloran, Michael 52
O'Hare, Dessie (Border Fox) 3–4, 85–6
O'Higgins, Kevin 41, 54, 55
OIRA *see* Official Irish Republican Army
Oldcastle, County Meath 47, 63
Omagh bombing 94
O'Malley, Ernie 16
Omeath, County Louth 76
O'Rawe, Richard 79–80
Organised Crime Task Force 4
O'Rourke, Joseph 50
Ovens and Richardson store, Ballyconnell, County Cavan 47

Paisley, Ian 104
peace process 4, 87, 94, 102–4, 106
Peaky Blinders 5
Phelan, James 52–3
PIRA *see* Provisional Irish Republican Army
Plant, George 55–6
Plant, James 55–6
Player Wills factory raid 64–5
poitín-making suppressed 17–18, 32
Portlaoise prison 110
Portroe church, Nenagh 48
post office raids 14, 20, 27, 28, 40, 42, 46–7, 48, 53, 63, 64, 76, 77–8, 83, 85, 86
Pratley, Michael 50
Price, Dolours 76
Price, Marian 76
protection payments 1, 49, 81
Protective Corps 49
Protestants, sectarian animosity towards 43
Provisional Irish Republican Army (PIRA) 5–6, 7, 69, 72, 74, 75, 76, 78, 81, 82, 83, 84, 85, 90, 91, 93, 94, 95, 98, 99, 100, 102, 103, 105–6, 109

launch attack on Official IRA
(1975) 94–5
move against IPLO 98–9
threaten Saor Éire 75
see also Irish Republican Army
Public Safety Act 60

Quaid, Seamus 83
Quinn, John 16
Quinn, Paul 104–5

RAAD see Republican Action
Against Drugs
Rathdrum, County Wicklow 68
Real IRA 2, 3, 103, 106, 110
Redican, James 28
Redican, Thomas 28
Regency Hotel attack 109
Republican Action Against Drugs
(RAAD) 106
Republican Congress 60
Republican Sinn Féin 111
Reynolds, John 52
Reynolds, Michael 82
Reynolds, Patrick 85
RIC see Royal Irish Constabulary
Riverstown, County Sligo 48
Rogers, Keith 104
Roscommon town 24, 52
Roundwood, County Wicklow 84,
85
Royal Bank, Drumcondra 67–8
Royal Barracks 37
Royal Irish Constabulary (RIC) 17,
21, 23, 24, 28, 32, 37
1919 boycott of 13, 14
Royal Ulster Constabulary (RUC)
68, 79, 90, 91
RTÉ 1, 73
RUC see Royal Ulster Constabulary
Russell, Seán 62
Ryan, Alan 2–3

Ryan, Eamon 82, 83
Ryan, William 47

St Enda's College, Dublin 55
Sands, Bobby 6–7
Saor Éire 68, 69, 70, 75
Schull, County Cork 20, 28
SDLP see Social Democratic and
Labour Party
Seawright, George 98
Second World War 14, 62
sectarianism 43
Shanagolden, County Limerick 19
Shanahan, Phil 29
Sheehan, Gary 85
Sheffield 31
Shergar 84
shops raided 7, 12, 14, 16, 21, 24,
29, 38, 39, 40, 46, 47, 48, 49,
63, 71
Sills, Patrick 80
Sinn Féin 5, 13, 27, 29, 72–3, 76,
84, 86–7, 94, 95, 99, 101, 105,
106
on Special Criminal Court 107
Skerries, County Dublin 20
Sligo town 38, 40
smuggling 4, 31, 95, 96–7, 104–5
Social Democratic and Labour Party
(SDLP) 95
Sons of Anarchy 5
'Sons of Dawn' 13, 21–2
Soviet Union 53, 54
Spanish Civil War 64
Special Criminal Court 77, 78
Stanford, Joseph 21
Strabane, County Tyrone 64, 109
Stradbally, County Waterford 42
Strandhill, County Sligo 48
strike action 23, 36, 39, 50, 61
newspaper production 61

Strokestown, County Roscommon 29
Sugrue, Denis 31
Sunday World
   Alan Ryan story 2–3
Swift, J.L. 46

Templemore, County Tipperary 42
Thurles, County Tipperary 77
Tidey, Don 84–5
Tierney, James 49
Tipperary town 55, 57
Tralee Post Office 76
Tramore, County Waterford 82
Treaty, the 36, 38, 40, 44
truce 36, 41, 45, 50, 53
Tuam, County Galway 22, 42, 50
Tuam Herald 22
Tullamore, County Offaly 47
Twaddell, W.J. 50
Twomey, Maurice 8–9, 54–5, 61

Ulster Bank
   Ballinamore branch 54
   Ballyconnell branch 47
   Monaghan branch 45
Ulster Special Constabulary 29
Ulster Volunteer Force (UVF) 101
United States 31, 32, 54, 56, 62, 63, 67, 82, 97

Vincent, Arthur 21

Walsh, Anthony 40
Walsh, Richard 31, 32
War of Independence 1, 6, 25, 52, 55, 110
war veterans and criminality 14, 24
Watchorn, Michael 52
Weston, Galen 84
Wexford town 44

Whelan, Eddie 62
Williams, Paul 2, 5
Workers' Party 72–3, 75

Yeates, Pádraig 27, 99
Youghal, County Cork 37